Preface

This textbook is part of a driver education course which was developed by the Ontario Ministry of Transportation and Communications specifically for use within the province's secondary schools in conjunction with complementary manuals for both the classroom teacher and in-car instructor. It is the end product of four years of intensive research and development involving comprehensive planning, evaluation, and field-testing as well as continual review and input from driver education teachers and researchers across North America.

Notwithstanding the fact that it was developed for Ontario, this textbook does not contain any specific references to or statements about Ontario laws and rules of the road. Instead, it uses examples of laws applicable across Canada and refers students to the appropriate provincial driver's guide or handbook for more detailed information when necessary. As well as accommodating students in other provinces, this technique has the added advantage of ensuring that information students receive about specific laws will always be up-to-date. As a result, when used in conjunction with the proper provincial handbook, this text is suitable for all Canadian students and should be so for many years to come.

This driver education course concentrates on attitude and skill development as the major means of ensuring safe driving performance. From the outset, students are encouraged to become *responsible drivers* who have a very low tolerance for risk. They are also taught the art of *strategic driving*: a complex set of driving skills which complements the notion of the responsible driver and emphasizes hazard search, detection, and avoidance.

It is hoped that through these lessons new drivers will come to recognize and respect the risks in driving and will consequently place themselves on a restricted driving career appropriate to the limits of their current skills in a dynamic traffic environment. However, as their skills increase, it is also hoped that their tolerance for risk will remain low: that is, that the attitudes to driving developed in this text will remain with them throughout their driving careers.

The text is divided into three units containing three chapters each. The first unit introduces the students to the basic car controls and manoeuvres. At the same time, the students learn what it means to be a responsible driver. The second unit teaches students about driving on various roadways including city streets, highways, country roads and freeways. Here they learn about strategic driving and how the skills it entails apply in different driving situations. The third and final unit discusses the problems and risks associated with nighttime driving, inclement weather, driver impairment, and mechanical failure, consolidating the attitudes and skills introduced in the first two units.

Although this textbook is a comprehensive guide to safe driving, we recognize that it cannot, by itself, teach students to be responsible drivers. This can only come about through the commitment of dedicated teachers together with the help and support of relatives and friends who are willing to give the students opportunities to practise the skills they are learning in class. Nevertheless, with a concerted effort on the part of all those involved, not the least of whom are the students themselves, our new drivers should look forward to safe and rewarding driving careers.

Acknowledgements

In addition to the many Ministry of Transportation and Communications personnel involved in the development and production of this textbook, the ministry would also like to acknowledge the contribution of the Ontario Ministry of Education and the following educational and traffic safety researchers and organizations who contributed to the planning and development of the new course: Behavioural Team, Barry Bragg, Canada Safety Council, Energy Probe Research Foundation, Engel and Townsend, Hieatt and Associates, Robert Kenzie, Alan King, James McKnight, David Pratt, Alan Robertson, Social Policy Research Associates, Transport Canada and Gerald Wilde.

The ministry would also like to thank the following driving instructors and driver training organizations from across Ontario for reviewing drafts of the textbook: Antero Elo, David Baker, David Notman, Canadian Automobile Association Toronto Club, Ontario Safety League, Eric Owen, John Powell, Phillip Randell, William Pollock, Don Reimer, Lakeram Sukhu, Robert Vaughan and Keith Wallace.

Finally, thanks are extended to the following people for their contribution to the textbook production: *book design*–Carol Anhalt, *illustrations and cartoons*–Clarence Porter, *photography*–Sidney Tabak, *technical drawings*–Tracey Doyle, *word processing*–William Bowen.

Road Worthy

Ministry of Transportation and Communications

Ontario

Managing Editor	Linda Clifford
Editors	Gillian Bartlett
	Ed Blake
	Douglas Cowan
	Lawrence Lonero
	Kalle Vaga
Design & Production	Synergistics Consulting Ltd.

© 1985
Ministry of Transportation and Communications
Ontario
Printed and bound in Canada
ISBN 0-7729-0017-5
Reprinted 1987, 1988, 1990, 1992, 1995
7th Printing 1997

Table of Contents

UNIT I: Behind The Wheel

UNIT II: On The Road

UNIT III: At Your Peril

UNIT I

Behind The Wheel

1

Becoming A Responsible Driver

In this chapter you will learn:

- *what you can gain from taking a driver education course*
- *the important impact which cars have in Canadian society*
- *about traffic laws and penalties*
- *what it means to be a responsible driver*
- *about legal safeguards for drivers*

The Benefits of a Driver Education Course

Your parents or an older, experienced driver can probably teach you the basics of driving. And certainly even if you take a driver education course you'll need to rely on them to help you get extra practice at the wheel. However, there are many benefits from taking a driver education course that you won't get from home instruction.

Driver education instructors have up-to-date knowledge of traffic regulations and practices. They will show you how to handle emergencies safely as well as teach you things about accident prevention, fuel economy, car maintenance, and alcohol, drugs and driving that you probably would never learn on your own.

In addition, professional driving instructors are specially trained to diagnose and correct problems new drivers are having before the problems turn into major difficulties. You will learn not only what you *must* do in terms of traffic laws, but also what you *should* do in order to become a responsible driver. This means you'll be less likely to have accidents.

But teachers and courses can never cover *everything* you may want to know. Don't be shy about asking questions or about asking your relatives or friends for extra practice sessions. Take your driver education course seriously. If you do, you will be on the road to a safer, more economical, and happier driving career!

The Car in Canadian Society

Over the last 20 years, the number of cars in Canada more than doubled. Clearly the car has a very big place in our society. Try to imagine what your life would be like if there were no cars or buses or trucks. It would probably be very different from the way you live today.

Most of us depend on road travel for getting to and from work or school, for going shopping, visiting our friends, or going on vacation. But if you stop and think about it, we depend on motor vehicles for much more than personal transportation. We also depend on them to get goods to the stores where we shop, to ensure our safety from crime and fire, and to deliver our mail. Our dependence on cars even affects the layout and design of our homes, towns, and cities.

The car is very important in our economy, too. Car manufacturing is one of the biggest industries in Canada, and in the world. And there are all kinds of occupations which exist because of motor vehicles. We need

people to design and build the roads, enforce the traffic laws, and repair and maintain our vehicles. In addition, people find work as taxi or bus drivers, parking lot attendants, truckers, and car insurance brokers.

In other words, the car provides us with many advantages. But our dependence on motor vehicles also has some major drawbacks. Every year there are hundreds of thousands of car accidents in Canada. One third of these accidents cause injury or death. There is also damage done to the environment through air pollution. The millions of kilometres of roads needed for motor vehicles disturb the natural landscape. Old cars which are no longer useful are difficult to get rid of and create "junk pollution."

So you can see, the car is a very important part of our society, both because of its advantages and because of its drawbacks. To reduce the harmful effects that cars can have, you as a driver have certain responsibilities. This means driving only when you really need to and driving as safely and efficiently as you can.

M.T.C. Ont.

Traffic Laws

All drivers want to reach their destinations quickly and without trouble. But because there are so many motor vehicles and so many kilometres of roads on which they can travel, there are bound to be conflicts. Therefore it is necessary to have rules and regulations to make sure our roads are both efficient and safe.

Traffic laws serve two main purposes. First, they help regulate the movement of traffic and so make our road system work. Second, they help prevent accidents. Traffic laws do both these things by helping drivers know what is expected of them and what to expect from others. For this reason you should always obey the traffic laws. Traffic laws can vary from one province to another, and even in some cases from one city to another. As a driver it's up to you to know the laws in any province or area where you drive. Being ignorant of the law is no excuse for a traffic violation. So study the province's driver's guide or handbook carefully.

The Creation of Traffic Laws

In Canada, traffic laws are made by all three levels of government: federal, provincial, and municipal. Federal traffic law is part of the Criminal Code of Canada, and applies everywhere in the country. Criminal negligence, dangerous driving, and driving while impaired by alcohol or drugs are criminal code offences. Provincial governments pass laws regulating driver licensing and the movement and control of vehicles, under provincial "Highway Traffic Acts." Local governments have power to enact specific traffic by-laws in their municipalities such as speed limits, parking, and prohibited turns.

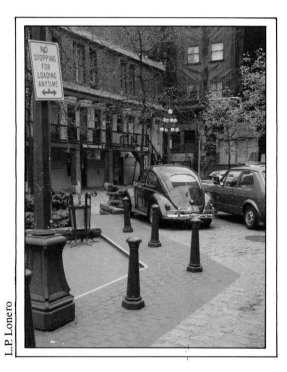

L.P. Lonero

The Enforcement of Traffic Laws

Several police forces are responsible for enforcing traffic laws. The RCMP have authority on all Crown lands such as national parks, and on most roads in provinces without provincial police forces. In some provinces, the provincial police enforce the laws on highways and expressways. Regional or municipal police enforce laws on regional roads and in urban areas. There are also some traffic officers (or "bylaw enforcement officers") who are not police but who can give parking tickets.

Police can stop drivers they see committing an offence such as making an illegal turn. They can use radar and airplane patrols to detect speeding drivers. They can also stop drivers simply to check the condition of their vehicles. In addition, the police can stop drivers whom they suspect have been drinking or are otherwise impaired.

Whether or not you think you have committed an offence, you must always stop whenever a police officer signals you to do so.

The Consequences of Breaking Traffic Laws

The severity of a penalty for breaking a law depends on the offence, the number of times you've been convicted before, and what the judge thinks of your attitude towards driving. There are two kinds of legal penalties for breaking traffic laws: fines and jail sentences.

Fines are the usual penalty for parking offences and "moving violations" like disobeying a stop sign or speeding. If you get a ticket for one of these offences, you can usually pay the fine by mail and avoid going to court. If you are convicted and can't or won't pay the fine, you may go to jail. For serious offences such as impaired driving, you have to go to court and you may get a fine plus a jail term.

In addition to these penalties, you could lose your driving privilege. Being allowed to drive is considered to be a privilege, not a right. The law courts and provincial licensing authorities can take that privilege away. For example, any conviction related to drinking and driving can result in your licence being suspended for three months or more as well as a fine and possible jail term.

Many provinces have a demerit point system aimed at detecting poor drivers and encouraging them to improve. Under this system, when you are convicted of a moving offence such as speeding, a certain number of points are recorded against your record. If you get too many points within a certain period, you may have to report to your provincial transportation authorities to explain your driving record and why your licence should not be suspended. If you continue to get demerit points, your licence will be suspended.

Some provinces also have a probationary driver system for new drivers who have just obtained their licences. Under such a system, a new driver is permitted to accumulate fewer demerit points before his or her licence is suspended. These probationary systems are designed to help new drivers correct any poor driving behavior before it becomes a permanent bad habit. The driver remains on probation until a certain period of driving without any suspensions has been completed. Then, like other drivers, he or she becomes subject to the general demerit point system.

Some Basic Traffic Laws

The basic traffic laws for each province are explained in the provincial handbooks and guides. You are expected to know all the laws for the province you are driving in. However, there are some basic guidelines to the general laws.

Keeping your driver's licence

The driver's licence is one important way of regulating drivers. Besides obeying the traffic laws, there are several rules you must obey in order to keep your driver's licence:

1. You must always carry your licence with you when you drive.

2. You are not allowed to lend your licence to someone else, or to borrow anyone else's licence.

3. If you move, you have to report your new address.

4. Your licence must be up-to-date. It must be renewed before the indicated date of expiry in order for you to continue driving.

5. If your licence is lost, you have to get another one.

6. You must follow any restrictions or conditions on your licence, such as wearing corrective lenses when you drive.

Obeying the speed limit

It is illegal to go faster than the speed limit posted on signs on the road you are travelling. In places where there are no speed limit signs, there are statutory limits. For example, in cities, towns, villages and built-up areas, the speed limit is usually 50 km/h unless otherwise signed. However, check your provincial handbook as this speed may vary.

Generally the more you exceed the speed limit, the higher the fine. Watch for places where the speed limit is lowered for a short distance, such as near schools or playgrounds.

Signalling

The law requires you to signal to other drivers whenever you stop, slow down, turn, change lanes, leave the roadway, or start moving from a parked position. You can signal by using directional signals or hand signals. Always remember to turn off the signal after you have turned or changed lanes. Leaving a signal blinking will confuse other drivers or pedestrians and therefore can be dangerous.

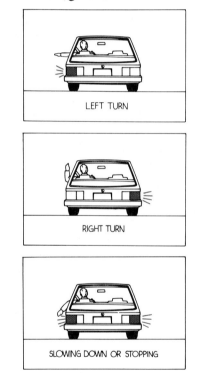

LEFT TURN

RIGHT TURN

SLOWING DOWN OR STOPPING

Directional signals should not be used to signal that you are stopped for an emergency. Use the hazard warning signals for that.

Yielding right-of-way

Right-of-way laws say who must yield; in other words, they tell which person has to let the other go first.

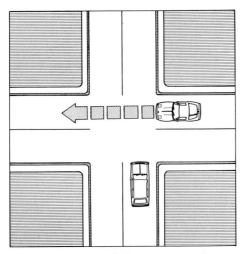

1. When two vehicles approach an uncontrolled intersection at the same time, the driver on the left must yield to the driver on the right.

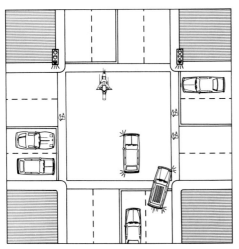

2. A driver intending to turn left or right must wait for approaching vehicles to pass and for pedestrians crossing the road on a green light, if they are close enough to present a hazard.

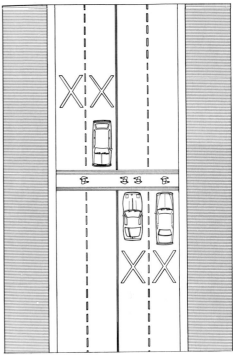

3. Drivers must yield to pedestrians crossing at specially marked pedestrian crossovers.

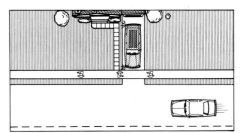

4. A vehicle coming onto the road from a private road, driveway, or laneway must yield to cars on the road and to pedestrians on the sidewalk.

5. Drivers approaching a yield sign must slow down or stop if necessary and yield to traffic in the intersection or to traffic approaching on the intersecting road.

Traffic Signals, Markings, and Signs

Traffic Signals and Markings

Everybody is familiar with traffic signals. But you may not know some of the special meanings of these lights for drivers. (Always remember that a police officer can overrule these lights.)

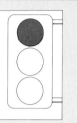

A red signal means that you must bring your vehicle to a full *stop* at a clearly marked stop line, or crossover, or, if there are no markings, just before the intersection. In most provinces, as long as you have come to a full stop and the way is clear, you are allowed to make a right turn on a red signal (unless otherwise posted).

A flashing red signal means that you must stop. You can then drive ahead only when it is safe to do so.

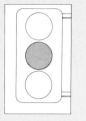

An amber signal *warns* you that the red signal is about to appear. You must come to a full stop unless such a stop cannot be made safely. If it is not safe to stop, proceed with caution.

If the amber signal is flashing, slow down and proceed with caution.

An amber arrow signal has essentially the same meaning as a circular amber signal except that, if you cannot stop, you may go through the intersection in the direction indicated by the arrow.

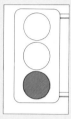

A green signal *permits* you to proceed if the way is clear. When making a turn on a green signal, remember that pedestrians crossing on the green signal have the right-of-way.

In some municipalities where traffic is congested drivers are not allowed to enter an intersection on a green signal unless they can be reasonably sure they can clear the intersection before the signal turns red.

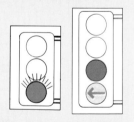

A flashing green signal or a green left turn arrow signal in conjunction with a green signal, permits you to turn left, right, or go straight through while the traffic opposite you is facing a red signal.

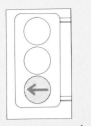

A green arrow signal means that you may proceed only if you intend going in the direction shown by the arrow. For example, if a left turn green arrow signal is shown you may proceed only if you intend turning left. If you do not intend going in the direction shown by the green arrow you must wait until a circular green signal or an arrow pointing in your intended direction is shown.

At some locations there may be separate signals to control certain turns and, if this is the case, there will usually be a sign to identify that signal. For example, left turns are on occasion controlled by a separate signal beside which there is a sign which reads, "Left turn signal." In this case you should obey the left turn signal if you are turning left, and you should obey the normal signals if you are turning right or going straight through.

Pavement Markings

Pavement markings divide lanes, show turning lanes, pedestrian crossovers, and obstacles, and tell you when it is unsafe to pass. Decide what you think the following markings mean. Then check them in your province's driver's handbook.

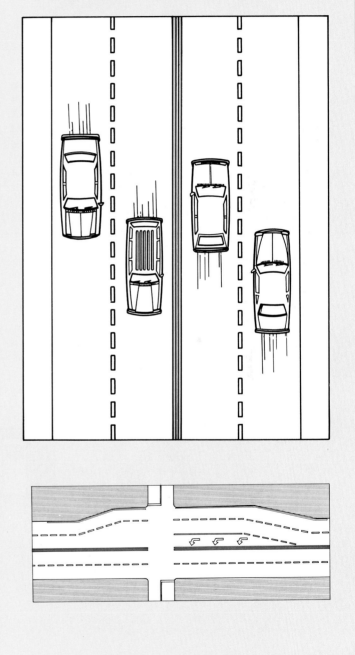

Traffic Signs

There are many different signs used to regulate traffic. However, these are not too difficult to learn. Most of them follow the colour-coding of the traffic signals. (And once again, a police officer can overrule these signs.)

Red circles with slashes through the middle prohibit or *stop* you from doing something. The figures in the circles represent the actions you are not allowed to perform.

Diamond-shaped signs in yellow *warn* you about road conditions or possible dangers. Just as with the prohibitive signs, these signs have symbols indicating the road conditions or dangers that lie ahead.

Green circles, like a green signal, *permit* you to do something.

 Signs that are *all* green with white letters or figures tend to give information.

There are many signs with different shapes and/or colours. Can you tell the meanings of the signs pictured below? Check your answers in your provincial driver's guide or handbook.

Responsible Driving

Having the legal right-of-way does not relieve you of your responsibility for avoiding accidents. Even if another person or driver has done something wrong, you can be found partially or wholly responsible for an accident if you should have been able to avoid a collision and didn't do so.

In other words, there is much more to driving than obeying the traffic laws, signs and signals. You must be a responsible driver, and that means learning to drive predictably, courteously, and artfully.

Driving Predictably

Because there are so many cars on the road today, driving is a very complex activity. Drivers need to co-operate with each other in order to keep traffic moving safely. In a sense, driving a car is like speaking a language. If everyone spoke a different language, people wouldn't be able to understand each other. In the same way, when you are driving, it is not good enough if what you do makes sense only to you. It has to make sense to other drivers too.

Driving predictably means doing what other drivers are expecting you to do. This means more than just obeying the rules of the road. For example, suppose you are driving in a heavy rain storm on a road where the posted speed limit is 60 km/h. The road is very slippery and most other cars are going a lot more slowly. Even though you might think you could drive at 60 km/h, other drivers would *expect* you to drive more slowly than the speed limit, just as they are doing.

But driving at a lower speed than the limit isn't always a good thing. In excellent weather and traffic conditions, other drivers expect you to travel at the posted speed limit. If you are driving very slowly on an expressway, you could hold up traf-

fic. Also, the car behind you might get too close to your car because the driver expects you to be driving faster than you really are. If you want to drive more slowly than the drivers around you would expect, you should keep to the far right lane and use your hazard warning signals.

In other words, predictable drivers drive according to the situation as well as to the rules of the road. This means doing such things as staying in one lane rather than moving back and forth, and signalling well before making a turn or lane change.

Driving Courteously

Responsible driving also means driving courteously. As you gain more driving experience, you will learn that there are many conventions of driving. These are generally accepted habits of polite driving which should be followed if traffic is to be orderly. Being polite on the road shows other drivers that you are thinking about your driving.

Responsible Passengers

When you carry passengers in your car, you take responsibility for their safety. You also have the right to expect their co-operation. Don't be afraid to tell your passengers where to sit or what to do. All occupants should wear their seat belts and a responsible driver ensures everyone buckles up.

Just like drivers, passengers in motor vehicles need to behave responsibly:

1. **Predictable passengers:**
   — sit so they don't block the driver's view out the rear window
   — give directions well in advance if the driver is unfamiliar with the route
   — wear their seat belts
   — don't move about in the vehicle while it is on the road.

2. **Courteous passengers:**
   — keep their conversations low and radios turned down
   — help the driver by reading maps, looking for addresses or street signs, watching for interchange signs on highways, and handling the change at toll booths or parking lots.

3. **Artful passengers:**
   — stop talking when some traffic problem arises that the driver must pay close attention to, such as turning or passing

   — look for and point out potential hazards if the driver doesn't notice them or they are in the driver's "blind spot"
   — watch for driver fatigue and suggest rest breaks on long trips or offer to drive.

When you are driving, your passengers can tell you a lot about how well you are driving. If you notice passengers holding onto the arm rests when you turn corners, you're going too fast. If they look worried or keep trying to point out dangers to you, you may not be reacting to hazards soon enough. In both cases, slow down and be more careful. At the end of a trip, the passengers are always a good measure of how well you've driven. If they are relaxed, comfortable, and didn't seem to notice anything unusual about your driving, the drive was probably a smooth one.

For example, in traffic jams or situations where two lanes of traffic are trying to merge, it would be courteous to allow other cars in if they have been waiting for a while. By taking turns in this way, two lanes can merge smoothly and quickly. Hogging the road doesn't really save any time and leads to conflict.

It is also common courtesy to give way to heavy trucks, if you can do so safely. Trucks are more difficult to manoeuvre than cars. In order to slow down, trucks must shift gears a lot and it takes time for them to pick up speed again. For this reason truck drivers will appreciate it if you let them go ahead first or give them an extra margin of space when you pass them. This is not only courteous, but also a good safety measure.

Bicyclists have a right to an equal share of the road too, so as a responsible driver you should be polite to them. Don't cut them off when you turn right. Stay behind them and allow them to continue through the intersection before making your turn. When you pass bicycles, give them plenty of room and pass them just as you would any other vehicle.

You should be courteous to pedestrians as well as to other drivers. At crossovers and intersections, pedestrians (especially children) are often uncertain whether a car will stop for them. You should stop well back from the crossover or intersection, but be cautious about waving walkers across. They should judge safety for themselves. Remember also to always signal well before you turn a corner; even if no cars are near, pedestrians need to know that you intend to turn.

Finally, being a courteous driver doesn't stop when you park your car; you need to watch out for other drivers even then. Don't block driveways, and avoid parking too closely to other vehicles. This makes it difficult for other drivers to get out. And when you open your car door, be careful not to bash the car next to you. You wouldn't like it if someone did that to your car!

Be courteous. Driving a car is often a frustrating activity, and small kindnesses are appreciated by everyone. Be courteous, but be reasonable. For example, you shouldn't brake suddenly to let a car enter traffic ahead of you from a parking space if a rear-end collision could result.

You will gradually develop this ability to do the best thing in each situation if you take your driving seriously and have respect for the other people sharing the road with you.

Driving Artfully

As well as driving predictably and courteously, a responsible driver tries to drive artfully.

Operating the controls of a car is a physical skill, but driving well is more than just that. It means using that skill to the best possible advantage at all times. It is, or can be, a real art. For example, skilled drivers know how to change gears and steer in order to keep their cars on the road. But artful drivers are more than just skilful. For instance, they know exactly *when* to shift gears on a hill in order to get the best performance from their cars. They know how to position their cars while driving so other traffic doesn't get too close.

Artful driving makes the roads safe for you, other drivers, and pedestrians. Every time you drive a car, you will encounter many hazardous situations but, by driving artfully, you will greatly lower the risk of one of these hazardous situations turning into a serious accident. Artful drivers are constantly alert, always anticipating hazards, and planning escape routes. They take pride in not having accidents — not even minor scratches or near-misses.

Imagine, for example, you are driving along a street and up ahead you see a pedestrian about to step off the curb. Some drivers would not notice this and would just drive along as usual. An artful driver, however, would slow down and be prepared to brake or move out of the pedestrian's way if necessary.

Artful driving has other benefits besides increasing road safety: it can save you money. If you are scanning the road in all directions for potential hazards and traffic signals, you will know well *in advance* when you need to brake. This means you will be able to slow down gradually, coast in gear, or possibly steer around hazards. Such actions make your brakes last longer and save fuel. In just the same way, artful drivers save fuel by accelerating smoothly, not jerkily. They also take corners and curves without tilting, squealing, or skidding.

As these examples show, artful driving involves precise control without sacrificing safety or courtesy. The fine art of driving is something you must learn through experience. You should start practising artful driving as soon as you get your learner's licence. When you are driving, keep watching for things that might cause an accident so you will learn to recognize hazards in advance. Never just shrug off a mistake — always work on it to make sure it never happens again. If you are ever involved in an accident or near miss, you should afterwards ask yourself why it happened and what you could have done to avoid the situation or escape from it.

M.T.C. Ont.

Traffic Accidents

If all drivers drove predictably, courteously, and artfully, there would be very few accidents. However the unfortunate truth is that the number of traffic accidents continues to be very high.

If you look at the number of traffic accident victims by age group, people aged 15 to 24 account for about 35% of all deaths and 40% of all injuries on Canadian roads. People aged 15 to 19 are more likely to be involved in car accidents than any other age group. An 18 year old driver is more than two times as likely to die in a crash than the average driver.

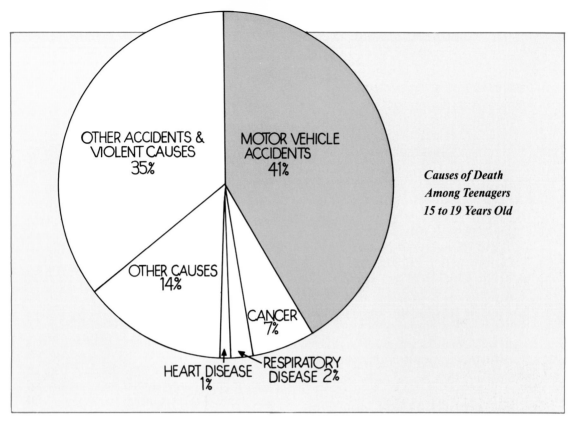

OTHER ACCIDENTS &
VIOLENT CAUSES
35%

MOTOR VEHICLE
ACCIDENTS
41%

*Causes of Death
Among Teenagers
15 to 19 Years Old*

OTHER CAUSES
14%

CANCER
7%

HEART DISEASE
1%

RESPIRATORY
DISEASE 2%

There are two main reasons why young drivers are more likely to have accidents — inexperience and an immature attitude toward driving. Even after you've passed a driver education course, there are still a lot of things you need to learn by experience. Learning to drive responsibly requires constant practice. Also, many new drivers — both young and old — haven't fully realized yet how demanding driving can be. They pay less attention to driving safely than responsible drivers do. The enjoyment of simply being *able* to drive can distract the attention of a new driver from the actual task of driving the car.

As a new driver, remember that your lack of experience and the novelty of driving may lead you to make unsafe decisions or to react incorrectly in an emergency. But if you are aware that this can happen and take extra care when behind the wheel, you can help prevent the accident statistics from including *your* name.

It is estimated that 80 to 90% of all traffic accidents are due to human error. And the most common types of driver error resulting in accidents are: failure to yield the right-of-way, speeding, loss of steering control, and following another vehicle too closely.

Alcohol is another major factor in accidents. About half of all drivers killed have been drinking. The drinking driver is much more likely to be killed than the non-drinking driver.

When you put two and two together from the statistics in this chapter, you can see that a new driver who has been drinking is running an increased risk. Young drivers are the most likely to have accidents, and drinking drivers are the most likely to have fatal accidents. *Young, drinking drivers* are really stacking the odds against themselves. If the law of the land doesn't get them, the law of averages will.

Car Insurance

Car insurance provides protection from financial loss resulting from an automobile accident, a loss that drivers would otherwise have to pay themselves. Driving without car insurance is illegal in Canada. If you are convicted of driving without car insurance, you may not be able to register your car. If you drive your car without insurance, you may be fined, you may have your driver's licence suspended, and your car may be taken away for a certain period. If you are in an accident for which you are responsible and you do not have car insurance, your licence will be taken away and you will have to repay the damages out of your own pocket. Claims for bodily injury could cost you hundreds of thousands of dollars.

How insurance works

Insurance helps a car owner pay for the costs of an accident. To get insurance, a car owner pays a certain amount every year. This amount is called a "premium." The amount of your premium depends on the amount of benefits you are insured for, the type of insurance you buy, and your driving record. Your premium may increase substantially if you are at fault in an accident.

One accident may cost the insurance company much more money than the amount you pay them every year. However, thousands of other people who never do have an accident are also giving money to the same insurance company each year. Insurance companies use part of the money from these premiums to pay for the costs of your accident. If the total number of car accidents goes up from one year to the next, insurance companies will increase the premium each person has to pay in order to cover all their accident claims.

Types of car insurance

Third party liability insurance. The most important type of insurance is *third party liability insurance*. This type of insurance is required by law in every province of Canada. Your liability insurance will pay for bodily injuries and property damage to others when you are at fault. However, this type of insurance will not give you any money if you are hurt or if your car is damaged.

Accident benefits insurance. Also very important is *accident benefits insurance*. This type of insurance coverage will pay reasonable medical or hospital costs to you or your passengers in the event of an accident. The insurance company will pay, no matter who is to blame. Accident benefits insurance is required by law, except in a few provinces.

Collision insurance. *Collision insurance* will pay for any damage to your car if it is hit. It does not matter if you were at fault or not. Collision insurance is generally not required by law.

Comprehensive insurance. *Comprehensive insurance* will pay for any damage to your car that was caused by something other than a collision — for example theft, fire, severe weather conditions, falling objects, and "acts of God." Comprehensive insurance is also generally not required by law.

As you can see, there are different kinds of car insurance. Different provinces have different regulations and options for each type of insurance. Find out what the requirements and options are for your province.

2 Getting To Know Your Car

In this chapter you will learn about:

- *the controls and other important parts of your car*
- *the outside and inside checks you should make before starting your car*
- *how to plan for everyday driving*

1867 Henry Seth Taylor Steam Buggy

The Development of Cars

Automobiles have changed a great deal since they were first invented. In the beginning they were simple machines powered by steam from a high-pressure boiler in the rear of the car. Unfortunately, these boilers could be quite hazardous. They could easily explode if the driver didn't control them carefully. In addition, these early cars broke down frequently. They were uncomfortable to drive, especially in bad weather, and only reached speeds of about 15 km/h.

Today's cars, by comparison, are complex, powerful machines driven by internal-combustion engines. They are equipped with a large number of features to make them reliable, safe, and comfortable. These range all the way from windshields and roofs supported by extra-strength beams to controls and gauges that tell such things as fuel level and oil pressure.

This chapter is designed to teach you about the basic features of the modern automobile as well as about the standard preparations and checks you should make before you even start the engine. You should be familiar with all the devices of your car and any other car you drive *before you drive it*.

Most cars have the same controls and gauges. However not all controls and gauges are found in every car in the same place, and not all of them look alike. For example, on some cars the headlight dimmer switch is a button on the floor while on others it is a hand lever. It is essential to know the location and use of the various controls so that you can operate them without having to look at them as you drive along. And the best source of information on these special features is the owner's manual written for the particular car you are driving. It is a good idea to remember throughout this book that you should always check your owner's manual for information on the specific procedures recommended for your car.

The Internal Combustion Engine

The internal combustion engine was first patented in 1860 by a Frenchman named Etienne Lenoir. This engine was ear-shatteringly noisy, but it caught on because it was a handy source of energy. Unlike the steam engine, it didn't have to heat up for a long time before it delivered power.

The internal combustion engine runs on a fuel like gasoline or diesel fuel. A mixture of fuel and air is burned rapidly inside the engine cylinders. The power from this burning forces pistons inside the cylinders to move. This movement then turns a shaft which transmits the power to move the vehicle.

There are two main drawbacks to this type of engine. The first is that it doesn't deliver very much power at low engine speeds. For this reason, cars driven by internal combustion engines need to have transmissions. These are complex systems of gears and shafts which maintain adequate engine speed when travelling at different road speeds. There is also a reverse gear which lets the car go backwards.

The second main drawback is the exhaust. These engines produce many poisonous gases which endanger not only our health but also our environment. Therefore, car manufacturers are required by federal government standards to add emission control devices to cut down on this pollution.

The Four Stroke Cycle

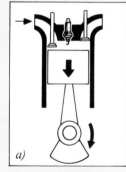

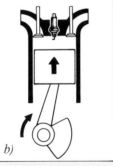

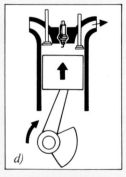

Intake Stroke

As the piston moves down, the air-fuel mixture is drawn into the cylinder through the intake valve.

Compression Stroke

The piston moves up and compresses the air-fuel mixture. (The intake and exhaust valves are both closed.)

Power Stroke

A spark ignites the compressed fuel-air mixture. This pushes down the piston, which turns the crankshaft.

Exhaust Stroke

The piston moves up and forces the burned gases out through the exhaust valve. The cycle begins again.

Operation Devices and Features

There are many devices and features which allow the driver to operate the car. These can be grouped into four main categories: *control*, *visibility*, *communication*, and *information*.

Control

The devices and features in this group allow the driver to start and stop the car, and to control its speed and direction.

Ignition switch

The ignition switch, located on the steering column or just beside it, starts the engine. There can be four or five positions on the ignition switch depending on the type of vehicle:

1. **lock**—locks the steering wheel in place so it cannot turn the wheels

2. **off**—stops the engine

3. **accessory**—allows the driver to turn on the radio and other electrical equipment without turning on the engine

4. **on**—normal running position—also turns on the gauges and indicator lights and allows the driver to verify that they work before starting

5. **start**—cranks the engine to start it.

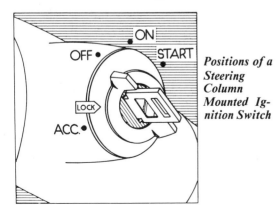

Positions of a Steering Column Mounted Ignition Switch

Steering wheel

The steering wheel is connected through a shaft and linkage to the two front wheels. By turning the steering wheel the driver controls the direction of the car. A car can have either manual or power steering. With the power system you don't need to apply as much force in turning the steering wheel as you do with manual steering.

If the engine on a power-steering equipped car stalls, the steering will still work, but the power assist will decrease and more effort will be needed to steer the car.

Accelerator or gas pedal

The accelerator or gas pedal controls the amount of power that the engine produces. This, in turn, controls the speed of your car. The farther you press down on the gas pedal, the faster the car will go.

Brake pedal

Brakes slow the car down and can bring it to a stop by placing drag on all four wheels. As with the steering system, it is possible to have either manual or power-assisted brakes. Power-assisted brakes make stopping easier because you are able to apply more braking power with less pedal effort. However, power-assisted brakes do not shorten braking distance. If the engine stalls on a car with power-assisted brakes, the power assist will still work the first time you apply the brake, but will decrease for each additional time you brake and more pedal pressure will be needed to stop the car.

Kinds of Brake Systems

There are two major kinds of brake systems: *drum* brakes and *disc* brakes. Drum brakes use *shoes* that expand and rub against a *drum* to stop the wheel moving. Disc brakes use brake *pads* that contract and pinch a metal *disc* on the wheel like a pair of pliers in order to slow it down. It is possible to buy a car which uses both types of brakes or just one kind.

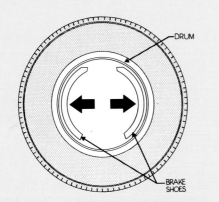

In a drum brake, the brake shoes press against the drum to slow down and stop the wheel.

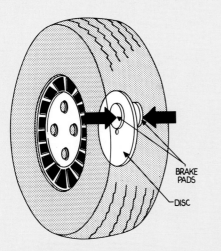

In a disc brake, the brake pads contract and pinch a metal disc to slow down and stop the wheel.

Parking brake

The parking brake is usually one of two types:

1. a small foot pedal
2. a hand lever next to the driver's seat.

The parking brake is used to keep the car from rolling when parked. It can also hold the car steady when starting on a steep hill. The parking brake operates only on the rear wheels. It is completely separate from the regular brake system.

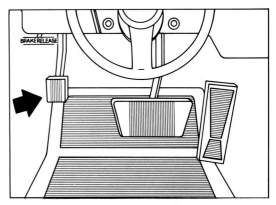

The foot pedal parking brake is engaged by pushing the pedal with the left foot, and is released by pulling the brake release handle located under the dashboard.

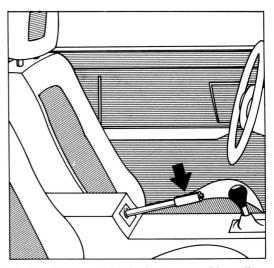

The hand lever parking brake is engaged by pulling up on the lever, and is released by pulling up slightly on the lever, pushing in the release button at the tip, and then lowering the lever.

Gear selectors

All cars have a transmission. This is the set of gears that sends power from the engine to the wheels. The transmission lets the car go forward or backward. Transmissions must "shift" when you change from forward travel to reverse, or when you slow down or speed up a lot.

An *automatic transmission* does the shifting work for you. This means you can go from low to high speeds without moving a gear shift lever. Some cars have semi-automatic transmissions. They automatically work the clutch but you must select and shift the gears.

On a floor mounted automatic transmission selector, the various gear ranges are selected by moving the lever forward or backward. To engage reverse or park, in most cars it is necessary to press a reverse lock-out button.

There are six basic positions for the selector lever in automatic transmissions:

1. **Park**—locks the transmission. This position is used when starting the engine and when parked, regardless of whether the engine is running or not.

2. **Reverse**—this position is used in backing your car.

3. **Neutral**—disengages the engine from the drive wheels. This position may be used when the car is standing still with the engine running, or when restarting the engine if the vehicle is moving when its engine stalls.

4. **Drive**—this position is for normal city and highway driving. The transmission will shift up and down as required. When stopped momentarily, as at a traffic light, it is not necessary to shift out of drive. Just hold the vehicle stationary with the regular brakes until ready to move.

5. **Intermediate**—this position can be used for either going up or down hills. It gives extra power for going up hills and extra engine braking for going down long grades.

6. **Low**—this position is sometimes used for driving through mud or sand, as it holds the transmission in low gear. It can also be used to climb a hill, or to slow the car when it's going down a very steep hill.

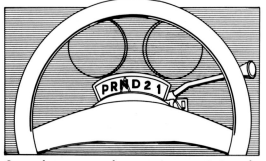

On a column mounted automatic transmission selector, the different gear ranges are chosen by moving the lever up and down. An indicator will show what range the transmission is in.

With a *manual transmission*, in order to shift you must press on the clutch pedal to disconnect the transmission. Then you smoothly move the gear shift lever to change gears, gradually let the clutch pedal up, and continue on your way.

Gear shift levers are found on the floor or steering column. The six basic positions for the gear shift lever are:

1. **Neutral**—the car is not in gear when it is in neutral. The neutral position is used to start the engine. It is always used whenever the car is stopped and the engine is running. This helps reduce wear-and-tear on the clutch.

2. **Reverse Gear**—is used in backing your car.

3. **First Gear**—this is a low gear for getting the car moving forward.

4. **Second Gear**—this is an intermediate gear. It is used for driving forward at moderately slow speeds, or for extra power or control on hills.

5. **Third Gear**—this is for driving in normal city traffic.

6. **Fourth and Fifth Gears** (on some cars)—are used for highway and freeway driving. Higher gears save fuel, providing that you are travelling at a high enough speed to warrant higher gear selection.

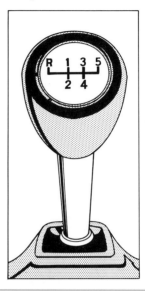

In cars equipped with manual transmissions, shift patterns, reverse engagement, and the number of gears vary. It is important to understand how to use the gear selector of the car you are going to drive before you start out.

Know Your Gear Selector

There are several kinds of gear selectors. Most manual shift cars have floor mounted selectors. Automatic transmission selectors may be found on the steering column or the floor.

Manual transmission selectors are standardized into a *H* pattern. Reverse gear is found in various locations. You may have to push a button, lift a ring, or push the lever against a spring to engage reverse.

To move a column mounted automatic in or out of park or reverse, pull the lever towards you as well as moving it up or down. With a floor mounted selector, you have to push a button to move the lever in or out of park or reverse. Be careful when you shift into drive that you haven't engaged one of the lower gear ranges by mistake. When shifting from reverse to drive brake to a complete stop before shifting.

If it is necessary to shift to neutral while the car is moving, be careful not to engage reverse or park. On column mounted selectors, push forward (away from you) and upward with the palm of your hand facing the dashboard and your fingers pointed up. With most floor mounted selectors, push the lever forward with the palm of your hand, but don't push in the reverse lock-out button. By shifting this way, you won't accidentally engage reverse or park. In some cars, where it is necessary to push the lock-out button to engage neutral, it may be risky to try to shift to neutral while moving because of the possibility of shifting into reverse or park.

Clutch pedal

The clutch pedal is found on manual transmission cars only. It is located to the left of the brake pedal. Your left foot is used to operate the clutch pedal.

This pedal operates the clutch which connects the engine and the transmission. When you step on the clutch pedal, the transmission is disconnected from the engine, allowing you to change gears. You should never move the gear shift lever from one position to another unless you have pressed the clutch pedal all the way down to the floor to disengage the engine from the transmission.

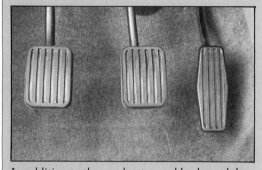

In addition to the accelerator and brake pedals, a manual transmission car has a clutch pedal located to the left of the brake. Always use your left foot to operate the clutch.

Choke control

Most engines have a *choke* or some means of helping to start a cold engine. It enriches the air fuel mixture. As with transmissions, some chokes work automatically. Most modern cars have an automatic choke. This regulates the air-fuel mixture without you having to do anything. Some chokes are controlled manually by the driver. You pull out the choke control knob to help start a cold engine. When the engine begins to warm up, you push in the choke control knob. As every car is built a bit differently, check the vehicle owner's manual for complete information about how the choke on your car works.

Visibility

Your eyes provide most of the information that you use when driving. Since a common excuse given by drivers involved in crashes is, "I didn't see him," you can understand how important it is to have a clear view of the road and traffic around you. There are a number of features on modern cars that help drivers *to see* and *to be seen*.

Windshield

The windshield allows you to see where you are going while at the same time it protects you from the wind, rain, and objects thrown up by other vehicles on the road. It is important to keep the windshield and other car windows clean at all times. In addition, there are a number of devices designed to ensure you always have a clear view of the road ahead.

Wiper/washer. Fluid from the spray nozzle of your wiper/washer sprays the windshield and allows it to be wiped clean. In the fall and winter, the washer bottle needs to be filled with special fluid that will not freeze. The bottle also needs to be checked regularly as the fluid is used up quite quickly. The time you find it empty is often the time you need your wiper/washers most.

Good wiper blades are also important. They, too, wear out and need to be replaced as soon as they start to leave streaks on the windshield.

Defroster. In cold weather the defroster dries off condensation, mist, and frost from inside the front window. The defroster also helps melt ice on the outside of the windshield. Some cars also have a rear- window defroster.

Sun visors. Sun visors can be tilted downwards and angled towards the windshield to keep the glare of the sun out of your eyes.

Some sun visors can also be turned to block sunlight from the sides. However, sun visors should not block your vision. Also, they should not be used to store things, which can later fall on your lap when you least want them to.

Mirrors

To handle your car safely, you need to know what is beside and behind it. Cars have an inside rear-view mirror for looking out the back window. In some cars the interior rear-view mirror has a nighttime feature which allows the driver to change the angle of the mirror so it does not reflect glare from the headlights of cars travelling behind.

Cars are also equipped with outside rear-view mirrors. These can be either flat or convex. The convex mirrors are made of curved glass. This curved glass increases the range of vision offered by the mirror, but OBJECTS SEEN IN THE MIRROR ARE CLOSER THAN THEY APPEAR. This is important to remember whenever you are relying on convex mirrors to tell you about objects behind your car.

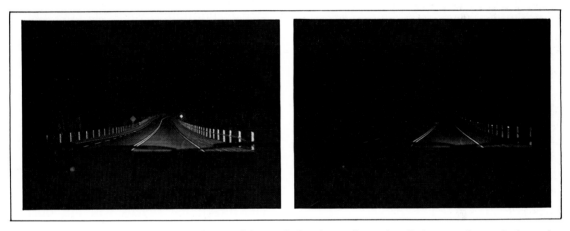

High beam headlights give you a good view of the road ahead. Low beam headlights must be used when other vehicles are present, but they don't allow you to see as far.

Lights

Lights on the car help you to see and help others to see you.

Headlights. The headlights are the most powerful and most important lights on the car. They can be switched to either high or low beam with a lever on the steering column or a button on the floor to the left of the pedals. The high beams help you to see far enough ahead for driving at moderate highway speeds at night. The low beams are used when other vehicles are nearby, because the high beams cause too much glare for other drivers. On cars not equipped with special daytime running lights, the low beam headlights can be used to help other drivers see your car more quickly in the daylight.

Tail, side, and dashboard lights. These lights are automatically turned on when the headlights are used. The tail lights and side lights allow other drivers approaching either from behind or across your path (as at an intersection) to see the position of your car. The dashboard lights, which should be kept dim at night, light up the switches and gauges on the instrument panel in front of the driver.

Interior dome light. This is a light used for reading maps at night or seeing inside the car. It should never be used while you are driving. This light goes on when the front doors of your car are opened, or by turning on a switch.

Communication

Communication devices allow you to tell other drivers what you are intending to do. These devices include your car's horn, directional signals, hazard warning signals, and brake lights. These parts of your car let you send messages to other drivers. Similarly, other drivers can send messages to you.

Horn

The horn lets you warn other drivers, pedestrians, and road users of possible danger. A light tap may mean "I am here." This would be used to make sure another driver knows you are near. A loud blast signals danger. It can be irritating and possibly dangerous to use your horn improperly— that is, to express anger, to scare another driver, or to say "hello" to a friend.

Directional signal lever and lights

The directional signal lever is found on the left side of the steering column. The directional signal lever is moved down to indicate a left turn and up for a right turn.

Appropriate lights then flash at the front and back of the car to let other drivers know that you plan to turn left or right or change lanes.

There are directional signal indicators on instrument panels. They will flash to show that a directional signal is on. After your car has turned, the directional signal will cancel itself when the front wheels are straightened. If it continues to flash after you have completed the turn or lane change, it can be shut off by hand by moving the directional signal lever.

Hazard warning signals

Hazard warning signals are used to call special attention to your car. They should be used if your car is stalled or if you leave your car because of a mechanical breakdown. They should also be used to warn drivers behind you when you are driving very slowly, such as in poor visibility conditions.

They are turned on by a switch or knob located on the steering column or on the dashboard. Two warning lights at the front and rear of your car then flash on and off.

The directional signals will not operate when the hazard warning signals are on. It should also be noted that many hazard warning signals won't operate when the brake is applied. Many people sit by the side of the road with their foot on the brake pedal mistakenly thinking their warning signals are on.

Brake lights

Whenever you tap or press the brake pedal, red lights will come on at the rear of the car. This signals to other drivers that your car is slowing down, stopping, or standing still. Flashing the brake lights with quick taps alerts the drivers behind that you are slowing down.

Symbols are used to label the various controls and instruments on the dashboard.

Information

Every car has a number of gauges and lights on the instrument panel or dashboard. These tell the driver important things about how the car is working.

The gauges and lights are not located in the same position on every car. However, on most new cars they are marked by standard international symbols.

Fluid gauges and lights

There are a number of gauges and lights which tell you about the fluids in your car.

Fuel gauge. The fuel gauge shows how much fuel is left in the tank. The gauge is usually divided into five parts: empty (E), 1/4, 1/2, 3/4, and full (F). When the needle falls to the 1/4 mark, it is time to refuel. Don't wait until the tank is almost empty before refueling. Running out of fuel can be annoying and even dangerous.

Coolant temperature indicator. The coolant temperature indicator warns you if the water and antifreeze circulating in the engine is getting too hot. If the indicator needle or light registers "hot," the coolant is soon going to boil. Stop the car as soon as

possible and have the cooling system checked at a garage.

The needle or light will register "cold" when you first start your car. Once the engine is warmed up, it should register neither "hot" nor "cold." If the car has a coolant temperature gauge, learn where the needle usually points. Once you know the normal position, you will then know when the needle indicates the engine is too hot.

Oil pressure indicator. The oil pressure light comes on as soon as the ignition is turned to the "on" position, but goes off again once the car has started. If the warning light goes on or the oil pressure needle drops much below its normal position while you are driving, it means that your oil pressure is too low. Pull off the road as quickly as it is safe to do so and turn off the engine. If you drive the car any distance in this condition, you may severely damage the engine. Have a mechanic check the oil system.

Meters

Speedometer. The speedometer indicates how fast the car is going. Some speedometers have marks to guide the driver when to shift gears.

Odometer. The odometer records the distance travelled. It is illegal to reset this meter. Some cars, however, have separate "trip odometers" which can be reset to zero. These are normally used to measure how far you have travelled on a certain trip or how many kilometres you have travelled on a tank of fuel.

Tachometer. Some cars are equipped with a tachometer. This device shows how fast the engine is turning. It also indicates when to shift the transmission in order to avoid either wasting fuel or damaging the engine by making it turn too fast or too slow.

Warning lights

High beam indicator light. Your high beam indicator light is found on the instrument panel. This light goes on when you put on your car's high beams.

Brake warning light. The brake warning light normally comes on after you put on the parking brake to indicate that it has been set. If this light comes on while braking, there is something wrong with your brake system. Stop the car at the first opportunity and do not drive until the problem is checked by a mechanic.

Seat belt light and buzzer. If you have failed to fasten your seatbelt, a warning light goes on as soon as you turn on the ignition and a buzzer (or bell or voice, in some cars) sounds. The seat belt buzzer and light are reminders that you should never drive without having your seat belt on. The light and buzzer will stop after a few seconds. In some older cars they will continue to operate until you and your passengers fasten your seat belts.

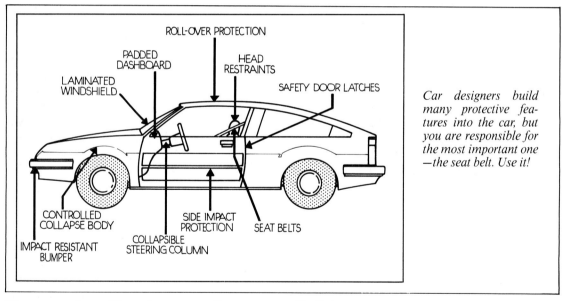

Car designers build many protective features into the car, but you are responsible for the most important one —the seat belt. Use it!

Protection Devices and Features

The modern car also has a number of devices and features designed to protect the occupants of the car as well as the car itself. These fall into the three main categories of *safety*, *comfort*, and *security*.

Safety

Every car has features which protect the driver and passengers from being hurt in case of an accident. Some of these are not controlled by the driver. For example, most cars have padded dashboards and side door beams. These parts protect the occupants of the car without the driver having to do anything. Other parts will give protection only if the driver or occupants remember to do something. Seat belts are an example. If they are not buckled, they can't protect you.

Seat belt

All new cars sold in Canada have seat belts. If the car hits something or stops suddenly, seat belts prevent the occupants from being thrown against the dashboard or windshield, out the door or window, or against other people in the car. In an emergency, seat belts also help the driver to keep control of the car by keeping him or her behind the steering wheel.

Head restraint

A padded head restraint is extremely important if your car is hit from behind. It is designed to prevent whiplash or neck injury when your head is tossed back in a collision.

Seat adjustment controls

The driver and front passenger seats on most new cars are equipped with levers or buttons which allow you to adjust your seat to fit your height and preferred driving posture. If you are not seated in the correct position, it will be more difficult to handle the car in an emergency.

Comfort

Air vents

Air vents are located on the driver and passenger sides of the car. These vents allow fresh outside air to flow into and move around inside the car. Fresh air keeps you comfortable and alert when driving in hot weather.

Heater

The heater keeps the inside of your car warm in cold weather. However, it is best not to keep the car too warm. It could cause you to fall asleep at the wheel. Some cars are fitted with controls that allow you to adjust the heat to keep your feet warm and your head cool.

Air conditioner

The air conditioner is helpful in hot weather. Staying cool will help keep you alert at the wheel. But remember that an air conditioner is a fuel-waster, especially in stop-and-go city driving. In the city, you can save on fuel by using the car's air vents or by opening the car windows in hot weather instead of using an air conditioner. However, very little additional fuel is consumed by an air conditioner on the highway where a steady speed is maintained.

Cruise or speed control

This accessory device is found on some cars. It allows you to travel at the same speed on the highway without keeping your foot on the accelerator. The speed control is activated by pressing a button on the steering wheel or at the end of the directional signal lever. By touching the button you can lower the speed of the car. By tapping the brake pedal you can release the device completely.

The speed control allows you to rest your leg when driving on the open highway. However, some drivers become less alert. They may start to feel too confident. Some may drive unknowingly into situations where they have to brake quickly. They may not be able to react fast enough because they aren't alert or their foot is too far from the brake pedal. For this reason the speed control should be used with care.

The Dangers of Carbon Monoxide

Carbon monoxide is a dangerous gas given off by all internal-combustion engines. It can cause headaches, nausea, dizziness — and even death. The problem is that carbon monoxide is odorless, colourless, and tasteless. This makes it hard to detect. There are some precautions you should take in order to prevent being poisoned:

1. Never start the engine in a closed garage.
2. Keep a front air vent or window open when driving, especially in slow, heavy traffic.
3. Always leave a window partially open when parked for any length of time with the engine running.
4. Keep the engine, muffler, and tailpipe in good repair. If any of these are faulty, they can leak carbon monoxide.

Security

A number of devices make it difficult for someone to break into your car or to steal it.

Door locks

Door locks keep others out of your parked car. Always be sure to lock your car doors when leaving.

Steering column lock

The lock on the steering column will secure the steering wheel in place when it is in the "lock" position. Neither the steering wheel nor the gear selector lever (in automatic transmission cars) will move until the key unlocks them. The key cannot be removed from the lock unless the switch is in the "lock" position.

Ignition key reminder

A buzzer, voice, or bell will go on when the key is in the ignition switch and the driver's door is open. This reminds you to remove your keys when you leave the car. It reduces the chance of theft and helps prevent you from locking your keys in the car.

Checks to Make Before Starting Your Car

Every time you use your car you should make certain checks before you even turn on the engine. Although these checks at first may seem complicated, you will soon find that they become an automatic part of driving.

Outside Checks

Before getting into your car, walk around it. Look for things such as rocks, bicycles, and balls that might be in your way. Also look for children playing in the driveway or street.

Next, check your headlights, tail lights, windshield, and rear windows. Make sure they are clean. When cleaning snow off your car, clear it all off, not just off the windows. And don't forget to scrape ice and snow off your outside rear-view mirror as well.

Always do a visual inspection of your tires before you drive to see if they have enough air in them. You will be less likely to skid or have a blowout if they are properly inflated, and you will also get better fuel consumption. Use a gauge to check the air pressure in your tires every week or so, or have a service station test them for you.

Inside Checks and Adjustments

Once you are inside your car, you should always:

1. Place your key in the ignition right away.
2. Check that all the doors are properly closed.
3. Check the windows. Make sure they are clean, and free from ice or frost.
4. Check for objects on the dashboard and rear window ledge that could block your view or fall off.
5. Adjust your head restraint and seat.
6. Adjust air vents, windows, heater, and air conditioner so you are comfortable. In cold weather, roll down the driver's window a little *before* starting the engine to prevent windows from fogging up.
7. Adjust the inside and outside mirrors.
8. And, finally, never forget to fasten your seat belt and have all passengers fasten theirs.

Seat adjustments

Sitting the right way in a car is very important for comfort and for safety. If you are sitting the way you should be, you'll find driving to be much easier. There are three things to check when you get behind the steering wheel. They are: the position of your eyes, feet, and hands.

First, you should sit high enough in the driver's seat to see over the steering wheel and hood. You should be able to see the ground four metres in front of the car. Use a firm cushion if needed. If your car seat has an adjustable head restraint, you should make sure it is at the right height. The back of your head should be directly in front of the middle of the head restraint.

Second, there is a tendency for drivers to adjust their seat too far forward or too far backward. This makes it difficult to handle the car in an emergency. In order to adjust your seat position properly, first be sure that you are sitting straight in the seat. A lot of new drivers don't feel comfortable unless their chin is practically on the steering wheel. Beware of this, but don't sit too far back either. Adjust the seat so your foot can reach the floor flat on the fire-wall behind the brake pedal. This will allow you to press on the brake pedal as hard as necessary. Your left foot should rest flat on the fire wall to the left of the clutch or brake pedal. This keeps you in the proper, upright sitting position and gives you more stability when manoeuvring your car.

High heels, platform shoes, and heavy boots can be dangerous when driving. Since pointed heels can get stuck under the accelerator, it is probably a good idea to keep flat-heeled shoes in the car that can be worn instead. You should be able to move your foot quickly from the accelerator to the brake pedal without difficulty.

Third, think of the steering wheel as a clock. Your hands should be placed where the hands of a clock would read 9 and 3, or 10 and 2. When driving in winter, you

Sitting properly is essential for good control of your car. There are three things to check when you get behind the steering wheel: the position of your feet, hands, and head.

should not wear wool mittens because they slip on the plastic steering wheel rim. It would be a good idea to purchase a special pair of driving gloves for winter.

Mirror adjustments

Mirrors should be positioned so that there are as few blind spots for the driver as possible. Blind spots in most cars are to the back left and back right of the car. On some cars the blind spot is so large that a car could be there and you wouldn't see it.

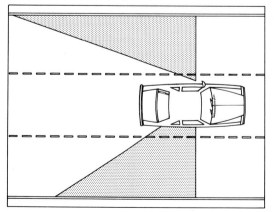

Turning your head to make a "shoulder check" is the only way to ensure that there is nothing in your blind spot.

To reduce the blind spots, position the interior and left-outside mirrors so there is no overlap in what you can see with them. You should be able to see directly behind the car when the interior mirror is properly adjusted. The left-outside mirror should be adjusted to give you a view of the rear left side of your car. Because your side mirror shows only a narrow angle of view, it will be necessary to turn your head to see if anything is in your blind spots.

You should know the blind spots on your own car. You can learn where and how large they are by having someone walk around your car and watching the person in the mirror.

Seat belt adjustments

Except for an alert driver, seat belts are the most important safety device in your car. The lap belt should be adjusted to fit snugly across your hips. There should be very little slack between the shoulder belt and your chest. Never wear a shoulder belt without the lap belt. This will give you little protection. When you fasten your seat belt, make sure others in the car do the same.

Planning For Everyday Driving

Your car can be a big convenience. But it should not be used more than necessary. This is for several good reasons. First, cars cause air pollution. The more you use your car, the more pollutants it will give off. Also, fuel is very expensive. Cutting down on the number of times you take out your car will save you money on fuel.

For everyday driving, you should keep several things in mind. Ask yourself whether you can get where you want to go without using your car. Would it be just as easy to walk or take public transportation? Once you decide to drive, planning is important. What is the best time of day to drive? What is the safest and most efficient route? These are important things to consider before getting behind the wheel.

Time of Day

You should think carefully about when to drive. It takes longer to reach a destination in heavy, rush hour traffic. Stop-and-go driving also means that you use more fuel. If possible, travel when there is little traffic.

Nighttime driving also presents a much higher risk. As it gets later, there are more and more drivers on the road who are sleepy or impaired by alcohol or other drugs.

Route

Before you start out, plan your route. Advance planning will mean a faster, cheaper, and safer trip for you. It will be faster and cheaper because you will know where you are going and short trips can be combined into one, thereby saving you time and fuel. It will be safer because you can think about driving without worrying about where you are going. Always keep a map on hand for planning your trips, but never try to read a map while driving. Have a passenger read it, or pull over to the side of the road first.

You should keep in mind that the most direct route is not always the best route. It may depend on the time of day. If you are driving during rush hour, a roundabout route may be better in order to avoid heavy, stop-and-go traffic.

Alternatives to the Car

Our dependence on the car sometimes makes us forget that there are other ways to get places. Which way is best depends on a number of things, such as how soon you need to be there, whether you're taking things with you, and the price of fuel.

Public transportation

Most cities have some form of public transportation, such as buses, streetcars, or subways. In a large city, the public transit can usually take you anywhere you want to go. Public transit is almost always cheaper than driving, and is very often quicker too. Also, the time spent behind the wheel driving a car may be all wasted. On a bus, you can spend that time thinking, reading, or just relaxing.

Taxis

If you occasionally go somewhere where the bus won't take you, travelling by taxi can be cheaper than owning, insuring, maintaining, and operating a car. Taxis let someone else worry about the driving,

cost relatively little for short trips, and help reduce parking problems. A taxi is a good way for people who have been drinking to get home.

Ride-sharing

For trips to school or work, ride-sharing is an excellent way to combine the flexibility of the car with the lower cost of public transportation. Instead of several people each taking a car, they all go in one car, take turns driving, and split the cost of the fuel.

Motorcycles and mopeds

Mopeds and motorcycles are an inexpensive way to travel short distances in the city. They are cheaper and more fuel-efficient than cars. They're also easier to park. However, the statistics show that they are not as safe as cars.

Bicycles

The bicycle is one of the most efficient means of transportation ever invented. It's very cheap, completely pollution-free, and an excellent source of exercise.

3

Manoeuvring Your Car

In this chapter you will learn:

- *about natural forces related to driving*
- *how to start the engine of your car*
- *how to get both an automatic and manual transmission car moving*
- *the techniques of driving along*
- *how to change direction*
- *how to park*

Natural Forces in Driving

Before driving in traffic, you must learn how to manoeuvre or control your car. This includes steering, accelerating, slowing down, stopping, turning around, backing, and parking. As a new driver, it is important to be able to do the basic control tasks first. They can be practised on quiet side streets or in offstreet areas. Once these skills have been learned, you can then start applying them on the road in city, country, and freeway driving.

As the driver of a car you are able to command a great deal of power and force. If you have ever tried to push a stalled car by hand you know that it takes quite a lot of force to start it moving. And if you want to stop the car you have to apply some force in the opposite direction. You could run around to the front of the car and push it backwards to stop it. Of course, instead of pushing to make the car move and to stop, you would use the car's controls to apply the necessary forces.

You don't have to be a physical sciences expert to be a good driver, but you do need to know a little about the physical laws of car control. The natural laws are just as important to a driver as traffic laws.

Momentum

A physics teacher will tell you that all moving objects tend to keep going at the same speed in a straight line until some force affects them. For example, if you hit a baseball, its momentum will make it travel along a straight path. However, a force, gravity, will have the effect of pulling the ball back down to earth. Another force, air resistance, causes the ball to slow down.

How much momentum an object has

depends on two things. First, there is its weight. An object that's twice as heavy as another will have twice as much momentum at the same speed. An object that's three times heavier will have three times the momentum at the same speed, and so on. Think of the difference between being hit by a ping pong ball and a golf ball.

The second factor momentum depends on is speed. An object going twice as fast as another of similar weight will have two times as much momentum.

A car can have a great deal of momentum because it's a heavy object that can move very fast. Once it's going it will want to keep going straight until a sizeable force is applied to turn it or stop it. To drive, you have to learn to work the controls to provide the forces to push the car along and to turn and stop it. You want the forces you control to affect the motion of your car, to make it accelerate, or turn, or stop. The motor, steering, and brakes develop the necessary forces.

Traction

In order for the forces provided by the motor, steering, and brakes to actually control the car, they have to be applied against something else. These forces have to be able to *push against* something. So unless your car is equipped with rockets, propellers, or some other unusual equipment, all the controlling forces are applied by the *tires* against the *road*.

The tires' main function is to apply controlling forces against the road: to push the car forward to go, or sideways to turn, or backwards to stop. Tires do this because of their ability to grip the road's surface. This is known as traction. Because they have traction, tires can push the car along, steer it, or make it stop, within the limits of the physical laws.

Up to this point the physical laws may not seem too important. Most drivers seem to get by most of the time without thinking about them very much. However, to understand the *limits of control* you have to think about the physical laws.

The limits to how much push the tires have can vary a lot. It depends on the car and the particular tires themselves. But most of all it depends on how sticky or how slippery the road surface is.

Most accidents happen because the driver has gotten into a situation where either the driver or the tires cannot control the momentum of the car well enough to avoid a collision. If the tires cannot provide enough push to turn or stop the car quickly enough, then you may have an accident. All your control of the car depends on the four little patches where the tires touch the road.

All kinds of situations will test you and your tires, everything from careless drivers pulling out in front of you, to your own mistake in getting into a curve too fast. If you have enough *traction*, and don't have too much *momentum*, you can save a bad situation from becoming an accident. Again, it all depends on those *tire patches*.

Of course, when you have had enough experience and developed good perception skills, you can usually avoid getting into bad situations in the first place. Until you get that good, it's just you and your tires, trying to keep on the right side of the natural laws. If you violate the laws of physics, you're going to be in trouble for sure, because you get caught every time.

Starting the Engine

The very first basic driving skill you must learn is how to start your car's engine. Remember that as part of starting the engine you should always carry out the regular outside and inside checks of your car. These checks include looking around the car for things that might get in your path, adjusting your seat and mirrors, and fastening your seat belt.

Basic Procedure

Starting the engine of a manual transmission car is not very different from the procedure for an automatic car. For both types of cars, do the following:

1. Be sure that the parking brake is set.
2. For an automatic transmission car, set the selector lever in *park* or *neutral*. For a manual transmission car, press on the clutch with your left foot and set the gear shift in *neutral*. Keep holding the clutch down.
3. To start the engine, turn the ignition key clockwise to *start*. As soon as the engine has started, release the key. The starting procedure is usually different if the engine is cold than when it is hot. There are also different starting procedures for different types of engines. Consult the owner's manual to learn the correct procedure for the car you are driving.
4. After the engine is started, check to make sure that the gauges on the dashboard are working and reading "normal." Is there enough fuel in the car?
5. Try not to let the engine idle for longer than 30 seconds in order to warm it up. Idling wastes fuel and unnecessarily pollutes the air. In addition *gentle* acceleration and slow driving warm up a cold engine faster than idling in the driveway.

In some cars you can give the gas pedal a quick tap in order to release the fast idle mechanism once the engine is beginning to warm up. Once again, consult the driver's manual for your specific car to find out how your car's fast idle or cold start mechanism operates.

Starting a Cold Engine in Cold Weather

Many cars have special starting procedures for starting a cold engine in cold weather. Check the vehicle owner's manual for any special instructions. In any case, it may be difficult to start your car in winter because the temperature of the engine is so low. To make starting easier, many people use block heaters to warm up the engine before attempting to start. Block heaters may be used with timers which automatically turn on the heat several hours before the car is to be used.

If you do not have a block heater and your car's engine is very cold, in many cars you should push the gas pedal to the floor and release it once or twice before following the everyday procedures for starting a car. This activates the automatic choke. Once again, don't let the car's engine idle for too long a time. Start driving and let the car warm up while it is moving, avoiding heavy acceleration or high speed until it is warmed up. Warming up while moving allows the entire drive train to warm up, not just the engine.

Some cars have a manual choke. If your car has a manual choke, pull out the choke control before you turn the key in the ignition. Turn the ignition key to *start*, but keep your foot off the gas pedal. Once the engine starts, release the ignition key. Then push the choke control part way in. As

Plugging in a Block Heater

every car is built a bit differently, you may have to experiment with the choke control the first few times to get it working just right.

Starting a Flooded Engine

If you pump the gas pedal too much, the engine may not start because there is too much fuel in the engine. If this happens, slowly depress the accelerator to the floor and hold it there while you turn the key. If this doesn't work, turn the ignition to *off* and let the engine stand for several minutes. This allows some of the fuel to evaporate.

Moving the Car

Now that the engine has started, you can put the car in motion. Since the steps for moving an automatic transmission car are not exactly the same as for a manual transmission car, they are described separately.

Moving an Automatic Transmission Car

To move an automatic transmission car, follow these steps:

1. Once the engine is started, press firmly on the brake pedal with your right foot.

2. Move the selector lever to *drive*.

3. Release the parking brake, but keep your foot on the brake pedal so the car won't move unexpectedly.

4. Look in your rear-view mirrors for traffic and pedestrians. Also check over your shoulder.

5. Activate the proper directional signal. This way other drivers will know you are preparing to move.

6. When the way is clear, take your foot off the brake pedal and press down gradually on the gas pedal. To save fuel, take about 10 seconds to reach 50 km/h.

Driving a Manual Transmission Car

When you drive an automatic transmission car, the transmission will shift itself. To go faster you just press on the accelerator. However, when you drive a manual transmission car, you must change gears by hand. This is done by moving the gear shift lever from one position to another. You will have to practise co-ordinating the clutch pedal with the gear shift lever and gas pedal. When they are co-ordinated, the car will move forward smoothly without straining or stalling the engine.

Learn to select the correct gear for the particular speed you are going. If the engine is "racing," you need to shift to a higher gear. If the engine seems to be "laboring" or turning over too slowly, you should shift to a lower gear. When idling at a standstill, for example at intersections, shift to *neutral*. Finally, be careful never to leave your foot resting on the clutch pedal. All of these precautions will help prevent damage to the clutch mechanism and transmission. Proper gear shifting will also save you fuel.

As you can see, there is a lot more to do when driving a manual transmission car. Therefore, you need to allow extra time for shifting gears when you slow down, stop, turn a corner, speed up, and pass. But with practice you will soon learn how to shift gears to complete each of these manoeuvres smoothly and safely.

Moving a Manual Transmission Car

Moving a manual transmission car is a little more complicated because of the clutch. With practice, you should not have any difficulty putting your manual transmission car in motion:

1. With the engine started and the clutch pedal pushed to the floor, move the shift lever to *first* gear. Hold the car stationary with the foot brake. Release the parking brake.

2. Look in your rear-view mirrors for traffic and pedestrians. Also check over your shoulder in the direction you're going to be moving.

3. Activate the proper directional signal. This way other drivers will know you are preparing to move.

4. Gradually let up the clutch pedal until it reaches the *friction point*. This is the point at which the engine begins to move the car.

5. Move your right foot from the brake pedal to the accelerator. Press down lightly on the accelerator.

6. Continue to let the clutch up gradually while pressing slowly on the accelerator. Your left foot should be on the clutch and your right foot on the accelerator. It takes a bit of practice to get the timing of your feet co-ordinated so the engine won't stall and the car won't jerk. The car should move forward slowly. Enter the flow of traffic carefully. To save fuel, take about 10 seconds to reach 50 km/h.

7. As you increase speed, you will need to change gears. When you reach the speed recommended by the owner's manual for your specific car, press down on the clutch pedal while letting up on the accelerator, and shift into second gear. Then let the clutch up and at the same time press down on

the accelerator. (You will need to repeat this procedure and change into higher gears as you gain speed.)

Starting the Car on a Hill

When you are starting your car on an uphill, it is likely to roll backward. For both automatic and manual transmission cars, you need to make special use of the parking brake to avoid this.

In an automatic transmission car, start the engine and put the car in drive. When it is safe to move, accelerate while releasing the parking brake.

With a manual transmission car, the parking brake should also be set before you start. Keep it on as you start the engine and gradually begin letting up on the clutch. Once you feel the friction point and have started to press down on the accelerator, you should release the parking brake. Continue pressing on the accelerator as you release the parking brake. Then continue on your way, accelerating slowly and shifting gears as necessary.

The scanning pattern can be quite complex in urban environments.

Driving Along

As you drive along, you will need to be doing many things at once. Most important, you will have to watch where you are going and what other drivers are doing. You will also need to steer the car in the direction you want to go. And you will have to be able to accelerate, slow down, and stop as necessary.

Using Your Eyes

When you are driving, your eyes should be very busy. You should never just stare straight ahead at the vehicle in front of you and ignore the traffic around you. Your eyes should be moving constantly in short, quick glances. The main difference between very good drivers and ordinary drivers is how they use their eyes. Good drivers glance in their mirrors every 5 to 10 seconds. In fact, as you are driving along, your eyes should not stay fixed on any one target for more than 2 seconds. It is important to know what is going on well ahead, to the sides, and behind you.

However, the first thing to learn about using your eyes is where you should look ahead. To steer smoothly, look up and ahead with your eyes aimed towards the centre of your intended path. Look at where you want the car to go, not at what you want to avoid. Don't use the side of the road, the car in front, or the centre line as your target. Look up into the distance where you'll be in about 15 to 20 seconds. Looking far ahead will let you anticipate in advance what's coming and improve your control of the car.

Steering Straight Ahead

Your safety on the road also depends on your ability to steer the car precisely. Even small mistakes in steering can cause serious problems.

New drivers tend to turn the steering wheel too much. Of course a certain amount of steering is required, even when you are moving straight ahead. To drive in a straight line, you must turn the steering wheel slightly if the car goes off course. These steering adjustments should be smooth and gentle, especially at highway speeds. As you gain experience your steering will become more or less automatic and much smoother. If it does not become very smooth, and if you find yourself making a lot of steering corrections, you are probably not directing your eyes far enough ahead. Looking well ahead will make steering easier and smoother. Keep your eyes aimed high and steer towards a point in the centre of your intended path.

Accelerating

Acceleration is an increase in speed. To reach a higher speed, you need to press down steadily on the accelerator until you reach your desired speed. The speedometer will tell you at what speed you are going. When accelerating, the ball of your right foot should rest on the gas pedal with the heel of your foot on the floor near the bottom of the pedal. Flat shoes give better control in accelerating than do high heels, platform shoes, heavy boots, or bare feet.

A good rule to follow when accelerating is to do it *smoothly*. Increasing speed gradually is safer because it gives other drivers a chance to see what you are doing. Fast acceleration may take others by surprise.

Gradual acceleration gives them time to react. It also gives you better control of your car and saves on fuel.

Maintaining Speed

A car travelling much more slowly or much more quickly than the surrounding traffic can be annoying and a hazard to other drivers. So, too, can a car that is constantly slowing down and then speeding up. Therefore it's a good driving practice to avoid such changes by driving at the *common speed*, or the speed of traffic flow around you. In this way your driving will be more predictable to other drivers.

However, don't feel pushed into going beyond the speed limit. Even if the cars around you are going over the limit, you should obey the posted maximum. Therefore it's a wise idea to check your speedometer frequently at first. With experience you will be able to judge the speed of your car without looking at the speedometer as often.

Slowing Down

Slowing down is easy in an automatic transmission car. You just let up on the accelerator and, if necessary, press down slightly on the brake pedal. Whether or not you use the brake will depend on how much and how quickly you want to slow down.

If you want to slow down just a little in a manual transmission car, release the accelerator and, if necessary, brake gently. However, if you are slowing down a lot but don't intend to stop, you must shift to a lower gear to maintain the new slower speed or be able to accelerate smoothly the next time you want to speed up again. Do the following:

1. Slow down by letting up on the accelerator or by braking.
2. Press down on the clutch.

3. Move the gear shift to the next lower gear.
4. Let up the clutch and, at the same time, press on the accelerator enough to match the road and engine speeds. If you do not speed up the engine enough when downshifting, the car may jerk when completing the shift.

Sometimes it is necessary to go more slowly, especially on hills, turns, in heavy traffic, and in poor weather or winter. But it is a common mistake under these conditions to slow down too little or slow down too suddenly. If possible, always reduce speed *gradually*.

Stopping

In order to stop smoothly under normal conditions, you must apply the brakes firmly and evenly, not suddenly or too hard. For everyday stops on dry pavement, apply steady pressure to the brake pedal. Just as the car comes to a stop, ease up on the brake pedal. Then press it back down to hold the car in position. In a manual transmission car, press on the clutch pedal and shift to *neutral* as the car comes to a stop.

Try to develop the habit of braking well *in advance*. This will prevent the need for sudden stops that can cause a skid or a rear-end collision. To be able to brake in advance, you need to be scanning well ahead. Looking ahead allows you to spot trouble early, make better decisions about what to do, and to carry out your decisions smoothly.

It takes the average person 3/4 of a second to step on the brake pedal when trouble develops. However, reaction time can be even greater if you are tired or in poor physical condition. You should drive more slowly at such times because it will take you longer to react in an emergency. Better still, if you are tired or not feeling well, leave your car at home.

Changing Direction

You will need to change direction, either to reverse, turn a corner, or turn around. All of these manoeuvres will seem quite easy once you have practised them for a while. You should always make a "shoulder check" before changing direction. This means glancing quickly over your shoulder through the rear windows to see if any vehicles are in your blind spots.

Backing

If you are moving forward and want to go backward, check for traffic to make sure the way is clear, then bring the car to a full stop. Shift into *reverse*. Keep your foot on the brake (in an automatic transmission car) or on the brake and clutch (for a manual transmission).

You may want to back in a straight line or on an angle to the right. In this case, you should turn your body and head to the *right*. This allows you to see to either side out the rear window. Put your right arm on the back of the seat. Put your left hand at the top of the steering wheel. Then turn the steering wheel in the direction you want the rear of the car to move. The car will move in the direction the steering wheel is turned.

If you wish to back on an angle to the left (such as when parking on the left side of a one-way street), you will need to turn your body and head to the left. Then with both hands, turn the steering wheel in the direction you want the rear of the car to move.

With the car in *reverse*, back slowly in the direction you wish to travel. To do this in an automatic transmission car, simply take your foot off the brake and press the accelerator slowly. In manual transmission cars, backing very slowly requires special use of the clutch. With the transmission in *reverse*, hold the clutch at the friction point while backing.

When reversing in an automatic or manual transmission car, keep looking up and behind until you have backed completely and stopped the car. Make short glances to the side for traffic. Don't leave any blind spots unchecked.

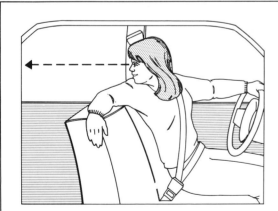

Look over your right shoulder when backing straight or turning to the right when backing.

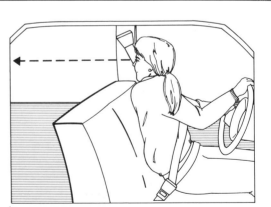

You must look over your left shoulder for a clear view when turning to the left while backing up.

Turning a Corner

In turning a corner you need to pay special attention to your steering and to your speed.

Steering

To make a sharp turn, you must turn the steering wheel more than half a circle. Use "hand-over-hand steering." Start with your hands at the 9 and 3 or 10 and 2 o'clock positions. One hand pushes the steering wheel up, around, and down. The other hand crosses over to grip the wheel on the other side. This hand-over-hand procedure is continued until the car has turned as far as needed. You should always have at least one hand on the steering wheel.

To return to the straight ahead after the turn has been completed, relax your grip on the steering wheel and allow it to slip through your hands. The front wheels should return to the straight-ahead position on their own. You may need to make a final steering correction by hand. Be careful never to let go of the steering wheel completely.

When you are moving very slowly or if the steering wheel does not return by itself, you will have to turn the steering wheel in the opposite direction to come out of the turn.

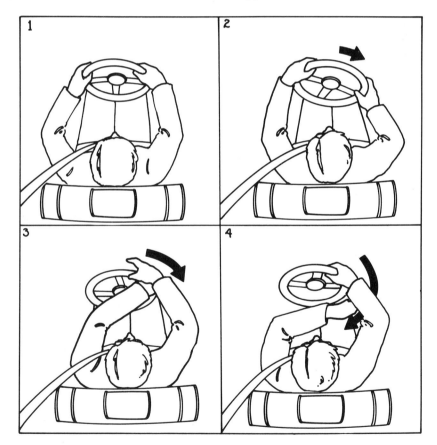

Hand-Over-Hand Steering

Slowing Down

The most common error in turning a corner is to approach the turn too fast. Turning the corner slowly gives better control. When turning at most intersections, you should not be going faster than 15 km/h.

You should slow down *before* your car enters the turn. Keep a steady speed in the turn. Then gradually increase speed as you complete the turn. Sharper turns require slower speed than gradual turns. Be careful not to hug the corner too tightly when you make a right turn or your rear tire will hit the curb. On the other hand, don't begin turning too late. This will make your turn too wide.

Turning Around

It is illegal and dangerous to turn around where you do not have good visibility of oncoming traffic, such as on hills or curves, or where signs prohibit such turns. Very often it is safer and faster to turn around by driving around the block. However, there are some places, for example dead-end streets, where you will have to turn around. Providing it is legal, choose a place where you can see clearly in each direction. Be sure you have enough space to turn around. Before starting to turn, check in all directions for traffic and pedestrians.

U-turns

U-turns are the simplest way of turning around. As the name suggests, a U-turn requires you to turn left across traffic and into the left lane in order to proceed in the opposite direction. Before trying a U-turn, check to see that there are no signs prohibiting U-turns, that the street is wide enough, and that there is no traffic coming in either direction. Make sure that you can be seen at least 150 metres away in both directions. U-turns should not be made close to intersections, hills, or crossovers.

To make a U-turn, do the following:

1. Mirror check to see who's behind and beside you. Signal for a right turn, shoulder check, and press gently on the brake to indicate that you want to stop.

2. Pull over to the right side of the street and stop. Check mirrors and blind spots for traffic. Then signal a left turn.

3. When there is no traffic in either direction, move forward slowly and then turn quickly and sharply into the left lane. Check for traffic as you turn.

U-Turn

Two-point turns

A two-point turn is used to turn your car around on streets that are too narrow for a U-turn. The best two-point turn is made using a driveway or laneway on the right side of the road. This way you don't have to back into traffic.

To make a two-point turn:

1. Mirror check, signal for a right turn and start applying your brakes. Shoulder check. Pull over to the right side of the road and stop your car just past the driveway.

Simple Two-Point Turn

Complex Two-Point Turn

2. Change into *reverse*. When the way is clear of traffic and pedestrians, back carefully to the right into the driveway, ensuring that the sidewalk is clear of pedestrians.

3. Stop the car when the front end is clear of the street. Then change into forward gear, check traffic, and signal to turn left.

4. Make a left turn into the street when the way is clear.

If there is no opening on the right side of the street, check the other side of the street for a driveway. However, this type of two- point turn is less safe because you must turn left across the path of oncoming cars and then *back* out of the driveway. This type of turn should be attempted only if there is no traffic in sight. Do the following:

1. Shoulder check, signal for a left turn and start applying your brakes. Shoulder check. When the way is clear, turn left into the driveway or laneway.

2. Shift into *reverse* and check both

directions for traffic and pedestrians. Back slowly and turn your steering wheel to the right.

3. Stop when the car is clear of the driveway. Straighten the wheels.

4. Check traffic and shift to *drive* or *first* gear.

5. Take your foot off the brake pedal and gradually accelerate into traffic.

Three-point turns

A three-point turn forces you to block two lanes of traffic. For this reason it should be avoided. However, a three-point turn may be needed if the street is too narrow for a U-turn and there are no laneways or driveways for a two-point turn. Before trying a three- point turn, make sure you can see clearly in all directions. Then:

1. Mirror check, signal for a right turn, shoulder check, apply your brakes, and stop on the far right side of the street.

2. Check traffic in both directions, and check blind spots. Then signal for a

left turn. When the path is clear, move forward and to the left. Steer towards the curb on the far side of the road.

3. Slow down as you approach the curb and turn the steering wheel to the right to straighten the wheels. Stop the car just short of the curb. Keep your foot on the brake and shift to *reverse*.

4. Check traffic in all directions. Signal to the right. When safe, back slowly, turning the steering wheel sharply to the right as you do so. Before stopping, straighten the wheels by turning them to the left.

5. Stop. Keep your foot on the brake and shift to forward gear. Check traffic at the same time.

6. When the way is clear, drive forward.

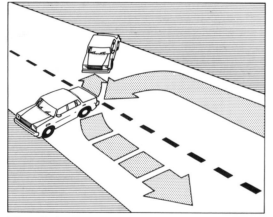

Three-Point Turn

Parking

Knowing how to park properly is an important part of driving. The descriptions and diagrams in this section will show you how to manoeuvre your car into angle, perpendicular, and parallel parking spaces.

There are two secrets to parking properly. The first is to position your car correctly before you start. If you haven't started from the proper position, you will have a very difficult time trying to get your car into the parking space. The second secret is to move slowly. This gives you time to make the steering corrections needed to manoeuvre your car into the centre of the parking space.

Once you are sure that you have parked properly, you need to secure the car. You do this by following these steps:

1. Set the parking brake.

2. Place the selector lever in *park* for an automatic transmission car. This locks the gears so the car cannot move. Also, in some newer cars, the selector lever must be in *park* before you can remove the key from the ignition. For a manual transmission car, you should put the gear shift into *reverse* or *first* gear. Keep your feet on the brake and clutch pedals.

3. Turn the ignition key to *off* or *lock* and remove it.

4. Release the pedal(s).

5. Unfasten your seat belt and close all windows.

6. Check for traffic before opening the door.

7. Get out of the car and take your keys with you.

8. Lock all doors. This will help prevent your car from being vandalized or stolen.

Angle Parking

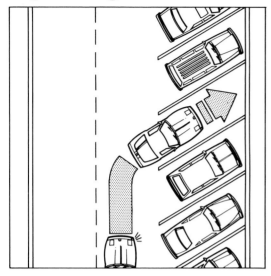

Angle parking spaces are often found in parking lots and shopping centres. The parking space is at an angle of about 60 degrees from the curb or a painted line. To angle park, it is awkward to back in. Therefore, you should enter front end first. Follow these steps:

1. Look out for traffic near the space you want to enter.

2. Check your blind spots on both sides. Signal a turn. Position your car about 2 metres out from the car parked before the space you want to enter.

3. Steer sharply into the space front end first. Move in between the lines of the space slowly. Don't get too near the cars on either side of you.

4. Straighten the front wheels as you move the car forward into the space. Stop when the wheels are near the curb or line. Be sure your car is centred in the space.

5. Secure your car.

In backing out, you must be careful to allow traffic and pedestrians to pass before you move out. Check your left blind spot and then the right blind spot for traffic behind. Then shift to *reverse* and move straight back. When your front bumper is lined up with the rear of the cars parked beside you, turn the steering wheel sharply. Once the car is completely out of the space, turn your steering wheel in the opposite direction to straighten your wheels.

Perpendicular Parking

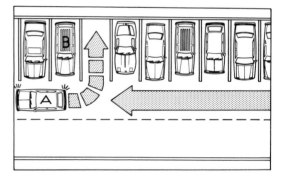

Perpendicular parking spaces are placed at a 90 degree or "T" angle from the curb or a line. Perpendicular parking spaces are found in many parking lots and underground parking garages. It is safest to back in. This way you will be able to exit easily. To perpendicular park, you should do the following:

1. Drive your car (car A) slowly past the empty parking spot you want to enter, about a metre out from the car parked beside it (car B).

2. Stop with the rear bumper of your car opposite the centre of car B.

3. Check your blind spots for traffic or pedestrians. Signal a right turn. When the way is clear, back up slowly turning the steering wheel sharply to the right. Watch that the left front-end of your car does not swing into other vehicles.

4. As you slowly reverse into the space, straighten the wheels so that you can position your car in the centre of the space.

5. Secure your car.

Leaving a perpendicular parking space is simple enough. When exiting, signal and make sure that your front and rear bumpers don't hit the cars parked to either side.

Parallel Parking

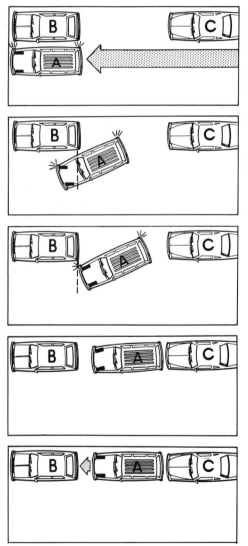

Parallel parking is the most difficult type of parking. It requires practice to do it right. First, you must make sure that the parking space is large enough for your car. You will need 1 1/2 times your car length. Then follow these steps for parking on the right-hand side of the street:

1. Check your mirrors for traffic. Don't stop suddenly if a car is close behind you. Turn on your right directional signal. Drive alongside car B about one metre away. Stop when your car's (car A) rear bumper is even with the rear bumper of car B.

2. When you have checked your mirrors and blind spots and are sure the way is clear, start backing into the space very slowly. As you reverse, you should steer sharply to the right until your car is at a 45 degree angle from the curb. Watch for front-end swing. Stop when your steering wheel is in line with the rear bumper of car B.

3. Straighten the wheels and then continue to back into the space. Stop when the right end of your front bumper is in line with the rear bumper of car B.

4. Turn the steering wheel sharply to the left as you continue to back slowly. Your right rear wheel should be close to the curb but not touching it. Stop the car.

5. Put your car into forward gear. Turning the steering wheel to the right as you do so, drive slowly forward. This should bring your car parallel to the curb. Stop the car when it is centred between cars B and C.

6. Secure the car.

If you aren't positioned properly the first time, pull out completely and start again. If you don't start correctly, it is very difficult to finish parking properly. Use the same procedure but reverse the steering directions when you parallel park on the left side of the street.

To move out of a parallel parking space, put on the left directional signal. You can increase your manoeuvring space by backing as close as possible to the vehicle behind. Check in all directions for traffic, especially to the rear. Check your mirrors and look over your shoulder. Steer sharply and move out slowly when the way is clear. Be careful not to hit the car ahead. You may have to re-position your car back and forth several times before it is completely out of the parking space.

Parking on a Hill

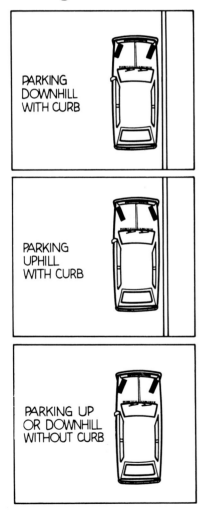

PARKING
DOWNHILL
WITH CURB

PARKING
UPHILL
WITH CURB

PARKING UP
OR DOWNHILL
WITHOUT CURB

The main problem in parking on a hill is making sure the car doesn't roll down the hill. The secret is to position the front tires so this can't happen.

Facing downhill

When parking with the car facing downhill, with or without a curb, bring the car to a parallel parked position. Move forward slowly, turning the steering wheel sharply into the curb or edge of the roadway. If there is a curb, creep forward until the front tire rests gently against the edge of the curb. Turning the front wheels towards the edge of the road prevents the car from rolling into traffic if the brakes become disengaged. Secure the car.

Facing uphill

When parking on an uphill with a curb, do the following. Bring the car to a parallel parked position. Turn the front wheels sharply towards the street. If it rolls backwards, the tires will catch the curb and prevent the car from going farther. When parking on an uphill without a curb, position the car in the space with the front wheels turned toward the edge of the pavement. If the car does roll, it will go off the roadway rather than into traffic. Secure the car.

UNIT II

On The Road

4

Driving
In The City

In this chapter you will learn:

- *how to drive strategically*
- *how to enter and leave traffic*
- *how to change lanes*
- *how to drive through intersections*
- *how to turn at intersections*
- *how to respond to special city vehicles and areas*

Driving Strategically

All of the manoeuvres described in Chapter 3 can and should be practised by learning drivers in deserted, off-street areas where there is no traffic to bother them. However, these are only the absolute basics of driving a car. Driving a car properly also means learning how to handle the vehicle safely and confidently in even the heaviest city traffic. You will do this best if you learn how to drive strategically.

"Strategic driving" is the use of certain strategies or rules of procedure when you are behind the wheel of a car. These driving strategies help you avoid conflicts and collisions with other road users. There are three key strategies:

1. looking effectively,
2. maintaining space, and
3. communicating.

By using these three strategies *correctly and together*, you will become a responsible driver: one who drives predictably, courteously, and artfully.

Looking Effectively

The visual system provides most of the information that drivers use to control their vehicles and to understand what is happening in traffic around them. The human eye is a marvelous instrument. Unfortunately, we are not born knowing how to use the eyes best for driving. In order to become really good drivers we have to learn to direct the eyes properly and use what they provide. It takes time, but with some effort the learning process can be speeded up.

You could think of the eyes as being like TV cameras. The eye and the TV camera both take in light and make it into a picture. They both send the picture on by means of electrical impulses. The TV camera sends its pictures over wires to a control room. The eye sends its pictures over nerves to the brain. The TV camera is moved around and focused by a camera operator. The eye is moved and focused by muscles. In the TV control room, a director tells the camera operator what to shoot, and the director also decides when to use the pictures from each camera. The eye muscles are told by the brain where to focus the eyes. And the brain decides when it will pay attention to the pictures that the eyes send to it.

However, there are some ways that the eyes are not like a camera at all. For one thing, the eyes make a very wide angle picture. Try this exercise. Hold a pencil in each hand. Fix your eyes on something straight ahead of you. Then hold your arms straight out to either side with the pencils sticking up. Keep your eyes pointed straight ahead. Can you see the pencils? Now wiggle the pencils. Can you see them better when they are moving? Vision to the sides, your "peripheral vision," is very sensitive to light and especially to movement.

Your eye is different from a camera also because the picture it provides is sharp and clear only in the middle. The sharp spot is really quite small. To demonstrate this, hold a ruler at arm's length in front of you. Keep your eyes focused on one number at the centre of the ruler. See if you can read numbers at the ends of the ruler without moving your eyes.

The brain mostly pays attention to the sharp middle part of the eye's picture. And it tells the eye muscles to aim the sharp focus at those things it's interested in. Fortunately, the eyes do not just wander around aimlessly. They move quickly between the spots the brain tells them to focus on. If the eyes are swinging past something that the brain recognizes as important, it will order the eyes to stop and take a clear look with the sharp part of the vision.

So most of the work of seeing is done by the brain. The simple part of seeing takes place in the eyes. But *seeing with understanding* takes place in the brain. It's your brain that really has to be trained to see efficiently. Books and teachers can help, but you will soon be on your own on the road. It normally takes years for a new driver to become skilled visually. You can speed that up if you try, but you will still have a lot of learning to do after you get your licence.

In order to get your driving vision to work really well, you have to learn to control your *attention*. There are a great many things that are important to the safety and efficiency of driving. The driver's toughest, and most important job, is to learn how to keep track of all the things that could be important. You have to train your brain to pay attention to the right things.

Unfortunately, the human brain can only really pay attention to one thing at a time. Therefore when you are driving, you cannot pay attention too long to any one thing, because something else can develop into a problem while you're ignoring it. You have to learn to keep switching your attention, and directing your eyes to check out all the different things that can be important.

Steering, speed control, navigation, road conditions, traffic and pedestrians all make demands on your vision and attention, sometimes all at once. You will be able to handle this because you will learn which things are most important and where to look for them. Your visual skills will become automatic, or habitual, after a while. Remember though, that sloppy, inefficient visual habits are just as easy to learn as good habits, maybe easier. You need to develop good habits so that your eyes will pick up important things around you even when you are not concentrating on your vision.

To develop good visual habits the first thing you have to do is learn to *look far ahead*. Even many experienced drivers are bad at this, so you have to make some effort to learn it. The second big trick in efficient vision is to develop good *scanning*, to keep the eyes shifting to check out all the places where something could be developing. Scanning, though, is not just letting your eyes drift around aimlessly. You have to develop a scanning pattern, and the pattern has to have a centre.

The centre of the scanning pattern should usually be up where you're going to be in about 15-20 seconds, or as far ahead as you can see. It's important to centre your vision way out ahead, so you can tell what is going on a long time before you get to it. This gives you plenty of time to decide what to do about some problem on the road. Looking far ahead also makes your vision *more* sensitive to where your car is pointed. This makes your steering control smoother. You can also see traffic well ahead so your speed control and choice of lanes are better. For instance, you can get advance warning of traffic stopping by checking the brake lights of cars well out ahead. If you just watch the car directly ahead of you, every stop is a surprise.

The second important thing in developing good visual habits is keeping your eyes moving in a sensible pattern. From your scanning centre (15-20 seconds ahead in your lane) your eyes must move to scan the sides of the road, to check the instrument panel, to check the mirrors, to look for road signs, etc. With experience you should be able to check these things very fast, in just a second or two. The sort of pattern you should develop is centre check, scan left, centre check, scan right, centre check, mirror check, centre check, instrument check, etc.

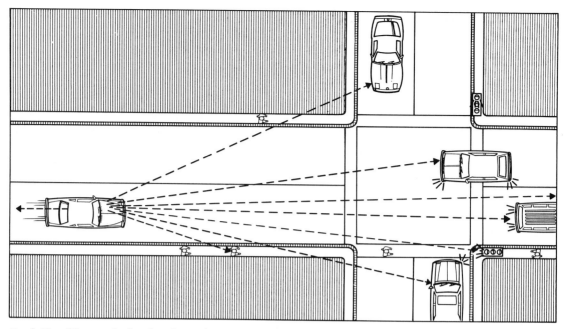

Look 15 to 20 seconds ahead and scan for important information.

The exact pattern, of course, will depend on the situation. For instance, if there is something special happening up ahead, say some activity on the shoulder of the road, then you would keep checking that between the other checks. A common mistake is to keep focused on one thing for too long. Your eyes should not stay on anything for more than two seconds. If it is important, keep coming back to it, but don't stop scanning as long as you are still moving. Some other problem could develop while you are concentrating on the thing that you think is most important at that moment.

You should look frequently to the sides and behind your car by glancing in the rearview mirrors. Be aware of your blind spots. Passing cars can be hidden from view there. You should always make a shoulder-check before changing lanes, passing, or making a turn. Two quick glances are better than one long one. Such checks could help prevent you from being rear-ended or side-swiped.

To best direct your attention and scanning

in any particular situation you have to use some *imagination*. A good driver learns to imagine, "What could be happening up there that I can't see yet?" With experience this should become automatic, so that you don't even have to think about it. When you are driving, things can pop out in front of you or emergency situations can develop very quickly. Most of the time though, there are clues that can be seen ahead of time. You have to check side roads, driveways, and every place from which something could move into your lane.

Where your vision is obstructed, say by a parked truck, you can still often see clues. Try to look *past* the obstruction, since it's what might be behind it that will cause you problems. You may be able to see the wheels of a moving car if you look under a parked truck. You might catch a glimpse of a child on a bike coming down a driveway by looking through a hedge.

City driving situations change every few seconds, so your scanning pattern will have to change frequently to keep up. If your imagination, attention, and vision are good enough, you will be able to handle these changing situations safely and efficiently, like a good strategic driver.

Maintaining Space

To avoid accidents, you should keep a safety gap or "space cushion" all around your car—ahead, behind, and on either side. The space cushion will let you see clearly in every direction. This will give you time and space to manoeuvre in order to avoid a collision. A space cushion will also allow other drivers to see your car clearly. They, too, will have room to avoid hitting your car in an emergency.

A space cushion in front

The greatest risk of a crash is *in front* of your car. Whenever you follow another car, you need enough space to stop safely in case the other car brakes suddenly. A two-second interval between your car and the car ahead is the minimum you should have. It allows you to see around the car ahead. It also allows you to stop in time if the car ahead brakes suddenly. To use the "two-second rule" on following distance, follow these three steps:

1. Pick out a fixed check point on the road ahead (for example, a telephone pole).

2. When the rear of the car ahead passes the check point, begin counting "one thousand and *one*, one thousand and *two*."

3. When the front of your car reaches the check point, stop counting. If you reach the check point *before* you finish the two-second count, you are following too closely.

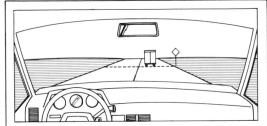

a) *The rear of the truck ahead has just passed the check point. Begin Counting.*

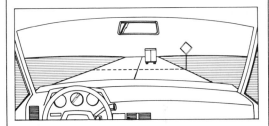

b) *Count: One thousand and one (one second).*

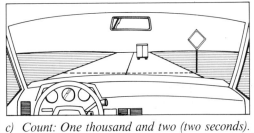

c) *Count: One thousand and two (two seconds). If it took less than two seconds for the front of your vehicle to reach the check point, you're too close. Two seconds is minimum. More time separation is even better.*

However, do remember that the two-second rule gives a minimum following distance. It applies only to normal driving conditions. In bad weather, or when you are following motorcycles or large trucks, or if you are carrying a heavy load, you need to leave more space.

A space cushion to the sides

Your car needs room *to the sides*. Try to keep a space of at least one car width to either side of your car. This will give you room to swerve if necessary to avoid something. When driving on streets with several lanes where you cannot keep a space cushion to the sides because of vehicles in the lanes next to you, be careful not to slip back into the other vehicle's blind spot. If possible, avoid driving in the lane next to the centre line, especially when oncoming traffic is heavy. This will free the left lane for cars wanting to pass or make a left turn. And it could prevent a head-on collision.

Although the right lane is usually the safest, try to keep a space between your car and parked cars. A car door may suddenly be opened or a pedestrian may run out unexpectedly from between two parked cars. Or a driver may start to pull away from the curb without seeing you. Sometimes there will be oncoming traffic on the left and parked cars on the right. In this case, you should "split the difference" and keep as much space as you can to either side of your car. In other situations you will have to keep your space cushion by handling one danger at a time. For example, if a car is coming towards you on the left and a child is riding a bicycle on your right, don't drive between them. Slow down and let the car go by first before passing the bicycle.

A space cushion to the rear

You also need to keep a space cushion *behind* your car. A common danger in city driving is "tailgating." This means a car is following too closely behind the one ahead. It often indicates that the driver is half asleep and is following the moves of other traffic like a robot.

If someone is tailgating you, change lanes if possible. If it is not safe to change lanes, slow down slightly and let the tailgater pass. Don't flash your brake lights on and off to get rid of a tailgater. This can be a misleading signal and is not likely to be effective. At the same time, be careful you don't become a tailgater yourself by following the car ahead too closely.

In maintaining a space cushion between your car and other traffic around you, never position your car in such a way that you have only one place to go in case of a sudden emergency. Try to keep several *alternative paths* clear for your car to move into. Think about where you would go if your present path of movement were blocked. In other words, try to keep your options open.

Keeping a space cushion ahead, behind, and on either side of your car will give you time and space to manoeuvre to avoid collisions.

Communicating

Many accidents happen because a driver doesn't see another car or because a driver changes speed or direction unexpectedly. Therefore it is important to let other drivers know that your car is there and what you are planning to do. In addition, you need to be aware of the messages other drivers are sending you.

Sending messages

Your car's signal lights tell other drivers what you intend to do. You must signal whenever you change position—for example, when you pull out of a parking space, intend to pass, or turn a corner. Similarly, your brake lights tell others that you are slowing down or stopping. When you press on the brake pedal, the brake lights at the rear of your car shine and send this message to drivers behind you.

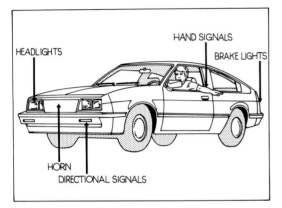

Sending Messages

Your horn is the fastest way of catching the attention of other drivers. However, it can easily startle them, so use the horn with care. A light tap can get the attention of a pedestrian, bicyclist, or driver who might not see you. A loud blast on the horn means real danger. For example, a child about to run onto the street should be warned this way.

Make sure other drivers see you. Visual contact with other drivers at intersections is essential. Drivers don't intentionally drive into other vehicles, they just don't see them. So be certain you see them—and they see you. Don't hesitate to use your horn or headlights to make sure you're seen. Use your signals. Be positive that your intentions are clear to others.

Receiving messages

Just as you can send out messages, other drivers can also send you information. The signals that other cars send out can tell you many things. The flashing directional signals of another car mean it is changing direction—for example, entering the roadway from a parking place or changing lanes. If the brake lights of a car come on, it means the car is slowing down or stopping. You must learn to watch for the lights on other cars, especially on the car ahead of you. This will help avoid accidents.

By looking carefully *in all directions* while driving, you can predict what others are going to do. For example, a parked car with a driver behind the wheel probably means the car is about to leave the curb or the driver intends to open the car door. To avoid these dangers, slow down and tap your horn lightly to warn that you are approaching. Or you can change lanes, but check first to see that it is safe to move left. Always *think ahead* about what others *might* do and drive accordingly.

While you drive, look out for warning signs of trouble. Watch out especially for:

1. other drivers who cannot see you—for example, drivers whose visibility is blocked at "blind" intersections, drivers backing out of laneways and pulling out of parking spaces, cars with snow-covered windows, or a car full of passengers.

2. drivers in trouble—for example, a car moving erratically (which may mean an impaired driver), or a driver trying to pass you who won't be able to overtake your car.

3. road hazards—for example, gravel shoulders, potholes, narrow bridges, school or construction zones, sharp bends in the road.

Each of these things is a warning that you should increase your space cushion by changing the position of your car or slowing down.

Moving In and Out of Traffic

The most basic manoeuvres of city driving involve entering traffic, changing lanes, and leaving traffic.

Entering Traffic

The most common way to enter traffic is from a parked position at the curb or from a driveway. When entering the flow of traffic, you must yield the right-of-way to cars already moving in the lane. Make an extra check for bicycles that may be moving in the lane. So you don't upset the flow of traffic, pull out from the curb only when you have a clear space for at least half a block. This space will give you room to accelerate up to the common speed of traffic without slowing down other vehicles. If the common speed is fast, allow yourself more room to accelerate and merge into the flow of traffic.

Before entering traffic from a parked position, it is important to signal your intention. A hand signal is often safer than a directional signal because cars parked behind may block your directional signal lights from view. Use *both* the hand signal and your directional signal light.

Changing Lanes

Changing lanes is a side movement from one lane to another lane on streets with two or more lanes in each direction. You may want to change lanes when the car ahead slows to turn at an intersection, in order to overtake another vehicle, or to avoid a parked car ready to enter traffic.

The steps for making a lane change are as follows:

1. Look in the rear-view mirrors for a space gap in the traffic flow that you can enter safely.

2. Check the blind spots for traffic by turning your head and looking over your shoulder in the direction of the lane change. Signal that you intend to move left or right.

3. Check the blind spot and mirrors again to ensure that the way is clear, and that no one is approaching quickly from behind.

4. Use a gradual steering movement to move into the new lane. Don't slow down—maintain the same speed or accelerate gently.

5. Once you are in the new lane, cancel the directional signal and check your new position on the road.

CHECK FOR SAFE SPACE GAP — CHECK BLIND SPOT & SIGNAL — CHECK AGAIN — MAKE GRADUAL CHANGE — MAKE SURE SIGNAL IS OFF

Changing Lanes

Never make sudden lane changes where you cut in front of another vehicle. Other drivers will expect you to continue using the lane you are already in. Even if you signal, they will expect you to yield the right-of-way to them.

Avoid unnecessary lane changes. They increase the risk of an accident. Don't change lanes where traffic is close together or near an intersection. Remember that wasting a few seconds behind another vehicle is often safer than going around it. And remember, bicyclists and motorcyclists are entitled to a fair share of the road.

Leaving Traffic

When leaving traffic to park at the side of the street, you must signal and slow down well in advance. Check your rear-view mirror. Give the correct directional signal. Then tap the brake pedal in order to flash your brake lights to warn other drivers that you intend to stop.

Be careful if you select a parking space after an intersection. Because you are slowing down and signalling, other drivers may think you intend to turn at the intersection. Therefore, don't signal until you are *in* the intersection. If you intend to park just before an intersection, signal well in advance.

Intersections

At intersections there is a flow of traffic and pedestrians in many directions. You must slow down and scan carefully in all directions.

Types of Intersections

There are two main types of intersections: uncontrolled intersections which have no traffic lights or signs, and controlled intersections which do. There are also "blind" intersections, which may be either controlled or uncontrolled.

Uncontrolled intersections

Uncontrolled intersections have no signs or traffic lights to regulate traffic. This type of intersection is found in suburban or residential areas where traffic is not too heavy. Because traffic is not regulated, uncontrolled intersections can be quite dangerous. Collisions often happen because one driver assumes that the other driver will stop, or that no one will be there. Another reason for collisions at uncontrolled intersections is that drivers don't even see them.

When two cars approach an uncontrolled intersection from different roads at the same time, the driver on the left must yield to the driver on the right. But if you are in any doubt, yield to the other car anyway.

At an uncontrolled intersection you have to judge the space between your car and other cars crossing your path. If this space is not big enough, you may not have time to cross the intersection without interfering with or hitting approaching cars. You need about four seconds to cross an intersection from a stopped position. Add to this a two-second safety margin. This means you must not start to cross if traffic is closer than six seconds away.

However, six seconds is a minimum only. If

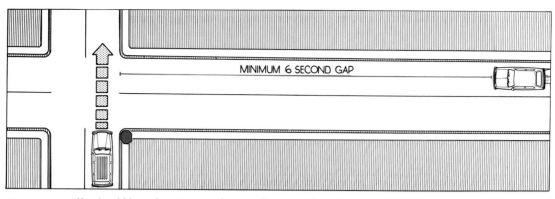

Oncoming traffic should be at least 6 seconds away for you to have time to cross the intersection safely.

the intersection is wide or the road surface is slippery, more than six seconds is necessary. If you find yourself in the very dangerous situation of *not* being able to see six seconds away either left or right, look and listen for clues of approaching traffic. Move a little bit into the intersection until you can see clearly. When the way appears safe, commit your car to crossing by accelerating quickly and moving directly across.

Controlled intersections

Controlled intersections have traffic lights or signs (stop signs or, occasionally, yield signs) to direct the right-of-way. For this reason, controlled intersections are usually safer than uncontrolled intersections—as long as everybody obeys the traffic light or sign.

As you approach any intersection, look to see if there is a stop or yield sign. If there is, you must obey it before proceeding. If there is a traffic light and it is green, continue carefully at the same speed. If the light has been green for some time, be ready to move your foot to the brake pedal so you can stop in case the light turns amber. However, if you are already so close that you cannot stop safely when the light turns amber, you may continue through with caution.

Blind intersections

As the name implies, at a blind intersection you cannot see clearly. This may be due to a building, billboard, tree, or other large fixed obstacle which prevents traffic approaching the intersection from being able to see clearly. If you cannot see clearly to the left and right as you approach an intersection, use extreme caution. The risk of an accident is high because another vehicle may appear suddenly in your path. Slow down and check carefully to both sides before proceeding.

Slow down and check carefully to both sides before proceeding through a blind intersection.

62

Judging Distance in Seconds

One skill every driver needs to learn is how to judge distance in relation to speed. The faster a vehicle is travelling, the farther it will travel before its driver has time to react to a given situation *and* the greater the distance that will be required to bring the vehicle to a stop. Thus, for example, a gap of 20 metres between your car and the vehicle ahead may be safe at one speed, but could be dangerously close at a higher one. You need to learn how to judge distance in terms of the number of seconds it will take your car to travel between two objects.

Practise judging how many seconds it will take a car to travel by standing at a busy intersection or beside a busy roadway. Pick out two objects—sign posts, mail boxes, even parked cars will do—one for the starting point and one for the finish line. Choose a car coming towards you and start counting seconds as it passes the starting point. A common way of doing this is to say "one thousand and *one*, one thousand and *two*, one thousand and *three*," and so on. Stop counting when the car passes the finish line.

Once you have counted the number of seconds it takes several cars to travel between the two objects, start trying to guess distances in seconds. For example, you may pick a car that you think will take six seconds to travel from the starting point to the finish line. As it passes the first object, start counting backwards "one thousand and *six*, one thousand and *five*, one thousand and *four*," and so on, until it reaches the finish line. The number of seconds that you are over or under "one thousand and *one*" will tell you how far off your guess was.

It takes a while before you can learn to judge distance in seconds accurately in different speed zones. Practise these techniques frequently on roads where cars are travelling at different speeds. Why not even start a contest with your friends to see who can judge the seconds best?

Turning at Intersections

Whether you are making a right or left turn, it is important to be in the correct lane well before you reach the intersection. You must be in the lane closest to the direction in which you are going to turn. *Never* turn from the wrong lane across another lane of traffic. This is a very unexpected move and is very dangerous.

You must also signal your intention to turn. Be careful, however, not to signal too far before the intersection. Other drivers may think that you intend to turn before you really do.

Once the way is clear you will need to make your turn slowly. Proper speed is important when turning. Your car should be moving at a slow enough speed that neither you nor your passengers are pushed sideways. Imagine a glass of water on the dashboard. Would it have spilled? Maintain a safe and constant speed in the turn and then accelerate gently after you have turned the corner.

Turning right

Right turns are easier to make safely than left turns because you don't have to cross an oncoming lane of traffic. However, in making right turns you still need a margin

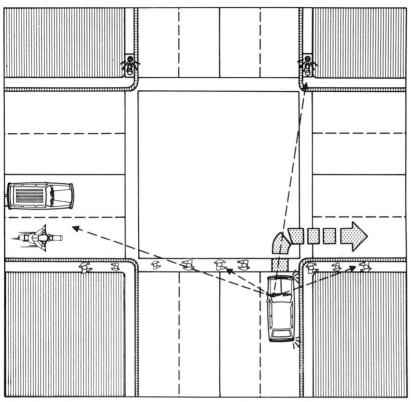

In places where right turns are permitted at red lights, you must bring your vehicle to a complete stop. You must yield the right-of-way to vehicles and pedestrians travelling with the green light, and proceed only when the way is clear.

of safety. Signal your intention to turn right well before the intersection. Approach the corner slowly.

Come to a full stop if the traffic light is red or if there is a stop sign. Yield to through traffic and pedestrians. Remember, intersections are the most dangerous place for pedestrians. Be careful, as well, of cars which might move suddenly into your turning path.

If the traffic light is green, you may be able to make a right turn without coming to a full stop. Nevertheless, always check first to make sure the way is clear and that there are no pedestrians crossing in the path of where you want to turn. Also, watch out for bicycles coming up on your right side and going straight across at the intersection. Don't pull up beside them to make a right turn, and then turn directly in front of them. Stay behind bicyclists and allow them to continue through the intersection before making your turn.

After you have checked left, centre and right, and made sure the way is clear, turn into the right lane of the intersecting street.

Turning left

Left turns are more difficult to make safely than right turns although the basic principles are the same; you must signal, slow down, and make sure the way is clear before proceeding.

To turn left you should be in the lane immediately to the right of the centre dividing line. As you approach an uncontrolled intersection or one with stop signs, you should signal your intention to turn and slow down. If there is a stop sign, you must come to a complete stop before proceeding. Look in all directions. Yield the right-of-way to traffic already in the intersection. Check again to make sure the way is clear. Then complete the turn.

When turning left at intersections controlled by traffic lights, signal your intention to turn well before the intersection. Slow down and scan ahead and to the sides for approaching traffic. If the traffic light is green and the way is clear, you can make the turn without stopping. However, there will often be oncoming traffic going straight through the intersection. You must yield the right-of-way to these vehicles. Move one-third of the way into the intersection and stop. While waiting to complete the turn, keep your wheels pointing straight ahead. This will prevent your car from being pushed into oncoming traffic if you are hit from behind. Complete the turn when the way is clear.

Some intersections have flashing green lights, or traffic lights with left-pointing green arrows, which allow protected left turns. When such an arrow is shining or a green light is flashing, oncoming traffic headed straight through the intersection is required to stop so you and cars behind you can turn left. Nevertheless, before making a protected left turn, you should still check to the left, right and straight ahead to make doubly sure the way is clear.

In all cases you should complete the turn by moving into the lane just to the right of the centre dividing line. The only exception to this occurs when turning left into a one-way street. In this instance, you should complete the turn into the left lane of the intersecting street.

Many motorists find it surprising to see bicycles and mopeds in left-turn lanes waiting to complete their turn. However, they are entitled to make this turn in the same manner as other vehicles. Therefore, if you're making a left turn and are behind one of these vehicles, don't pull up beside them and try to make your turn at the same time.

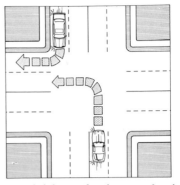

When turning left from a four lane to a four lane road, position your vehicle in the lane immediately to the right of the centre line well before starting to make the turn. Turn into the lane to the right of the centre line, being careful not to cut the corner.

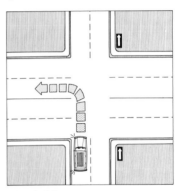

When turning left from a one-way to a two-way street, position your vehicle in the farthest left lane of the one-way street before reaching the intersection, and complete the turn to the right of the centre line of the two-way street.

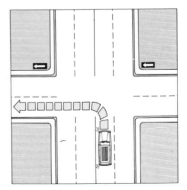

When turning left from a two-way street to a one-way street, complete the turn into the farthest left traffic lane of the one-way street.

Pedestrians

In cities, motorists share the streets with pedestrians. And just as there are poor drivers, there are also many careless pedestrians. Pedestrians can pop out in front of your car in parking lots, at intersections, or anywhere on the road. They may cross the street in the middle of the block simply because it's more convenient. Construction workers or delivery people at the side of the road may be more concerned with their work than with the passing traffic and may step unexpectedly into your path.

There are also pedestrians who require special attention. Small children, for example, are very unpredictable. They may run into the street in the path of oncoming vehicles without warning. And elderly people or those with disabilities may not see or hear cars well. They may also take a longer time to cross the street.

It's a rather chilling fact that in Canada pedestrians account for over 15% of all traffic deaths. Just remember when you are driving that you yourself are sometimes a pedestrian and would like to be treated with courtesy and consideration.

This is especially true when you are turning at intersections and driving past pedestrian crossovers. It is not only discourteous but also dangerous and illegal to cut a pedestrian off who has the right-

66

of-way. And never try to "race" a pedestrian in one of these situations in order to avoid having to stop.

Remember that pedestrians have the right-of-way at intersections when they are crossing the road facing a circular green signal or a "WALK" indication. They also have the right-of-way to finish crossing the road even after a circular red signal or a "DON'T WALK" indication has come on, provided they started to cross on a green or "WALK." The only time that pedestrians do not have the right-of-way when facing a circular green signal is when that signal is flashing green.

One of the best safeguards against accidents with pedestrians is to establish eye-to-eye contact. A pedestrian who isn't looking at you is certainly capable of stepping right in your path. It would be much safer if you were to catch each other's eyes. Nevertheless, this is no guarantee of safety. The pedestrian who is looking at you may be thinking "Ah, the driver sees me. It's safe for me to cross," while at the same time you're thinking "Ah, the pedestrian has seen me and therefore won't step out into the road."

Look closely at the photographs on these pages. Can you explain the pedestrian hazard pictured in each?

Special City Driving Conditions

There are a number of vehicles and areas encountered in city driving that require special care. In each case drivers need to be extra cautious and practise driving both strategically and responsibly.

Vehicles

There are many special vehicles which you are more likely to meet in the city than anywhere else. These include bicycles, motorcycles, emergency and large vehicles, streetcars and transit buses.

Motorcycles

As a car driver, you need to be alert to motorcycles. The biggest cause of motorcycle accidents in the city is the motorist turning left in front of an oncoming motorcyclist. As with bicyclists, a collision with a car is extremely dangerous for a motorcyclist. It is important to remember that motorcyclists need an entire lane to manoeuvre in. They have a right to that lane and you should not crowd into it. Also, on many motorcycles, turn signals don't turn off automatically. So, before turning in front of a motorcyclist, make sure the rider is turning and not going straight through into your path with a forgotten turn signal still flashing.

Some motorcyclists sometimes drive between lanes of traffic. Although this is a dangerous practice, you as a driver must be alert for motorcyclists on all sides and be prepared to give them extra room. Remember, as well, that motorcycles can stop faster than cars. For this reason you should always leave an extra margin of room in front when following a motorcyclist. Cross winds and sudden wind blasts from trucks can also force motorcyclists out of their line of travel. Be alert to these special conditions and it will prepare you for motorcyclists making possible quick changes in speed or direction.

Emergency vehicles

Ambulances, police cars, and fire engines use flashing lights and/or sirens when on emergency duty. At these times the emergency vehicles travel faster than normal traffic. By law they have the right-of-way. You are required to pull over as near as possible to the right side of the road (except for one-way streets where you may also pull over to the left). You must stay there until the emergency vehicle has passed. This gives the vehicles a clear path. In some areas it is against the law to follow closer than 150 m behind one of these vehicles when it is responding to an emergency.

Emergency vehicles have the right-of-way when on emergency duty and you must pull over as far to the right side of the road as possible until they have passed.

Large vehicles

Large and heavy vehicles such as trucks, trailers and vans can block your vision when driving along. Proceed behind them with caution and increase your following distance.

Remember that trucks are more difficult to manoeuvre than cars. This means you should give them an extra margin of space at all times. When trucks and other large vehicles make turns they may have to cut across your lane. Therefore, if you see a truck or bus signalling a turn at an intersection ahead, you should stop your car short of the intersection to allow the driver more room to complete his or her turn.

Transit buses

You need to watch out for pedestrians who are at or near bus stops or who are getting on and off buses. Approach a stopped bus with caution and give it an extra margin of space when passing.

When you see a moving bus full of people, you should give it the right-of-way. Remember, a bus is filled with many peo-ple. If all the passengers decided to stop using public transit and to drive their own cars instead, our roads would be hopelessly crowded. You can see it is only fair to let a bus in ahead of you in heavy traffic. One single bus represents forty or fifty cars you *don't* have to share the road with.

You will usually meet school buses on country roads. However you can also meet them in the city. When you do, be prepared to stop. More information about school buses is found on pages 74 and 84 of this text and in your provincial driver's guide or handbook.

Streetcars

Just as with buses, if a streetcar has stopped to pick up or let off passengers, you must stop your car at least 2 m behind the rear door. This rule does not apply when there is a safety island for the passengers to wait on. Nevertheless, be cautious as you pass a streetcar stopped at a safety island. A passenger may suddenly cross the road directly in your path. Never pass a streetcar on the left, whether it is moving or not, except on a one-way street.

Stop your vehicle well behind the rear doors of a stopped streetcar to safely allow passengers to exit and enter. Remember, pedestrians may be in a hurry and may not look before running to board the streetcar.

Bicycles

The bicycle is a vehicle that has a legal right to the road. The bicyclist, therefore, has the same rights and responsibilities as any vehicle operator and must follow the rules of the road. As a driver, you must take extra care to share the road safely with bicycles. Give them the same consideration that you give motor vehicles.

The most important thing you can do is learn how to look for bicycles and *anticipate* their actions, just as you would for motor vehicles. Because they are small and difficult to see, you must always look for them, even in situations where you do not expect to see them.

Wise bicyclists always follow the rules of the road. However, most are never taught how to ride safely in traffic. Many of them, especially children, do not develop proper riding techniques to ensure their safe movement on the road.

Sometimes they behave in ways that are not clear to you. It is, therefore, important for you to understand the reasons why bicyclists ride the way they do in different situations. This will make you more aware of potential car/bike conflicts. And it will help you avoid them.

The bicyclist is less protected and more vulnerable than you are in a collision. Be courteous, even if it takes a little longer. Remember, there is a fragile human being riding that bicycle.

Here are several situations that take special care:

Passing:

There may be road-edge hazards that you cannot see which will affect a bicyclist's ability to ride in a straight line— such as gravel, potholes, dangerous sewer grates, angry dogs, glass, or other debris. Wise cyclists will look, signal, and ride around obstacles, only when it is safe to do so. However, some bicyclists do not always do so, nor is it always possible.

Action: Give bicyclists as much room as you can when passing, even if they are riding close to the right-hand edge of the roadway.

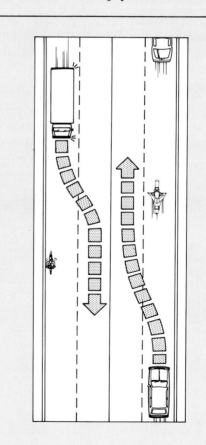

Many rural roads have unpaved shoulders. Bicyclists cannot ride safely on these. They will ride on the right side of the right lane instead.

Action: Allow ample room when passing a bicycle on a rural road with unpaved shoulders. Make sure the opposite lane is clear before passing in this situation. This is especially important when travelling at high speeds.

Turning left or changing lanes:

Bicycles are often travelling much faster than you think. Multi-speed bicycles can easily reach speeds of 45 km/h. Their speed is particularly difficult to judge when they are riding in the opposite direction.

Action: When preparing to turn left, make sure you yield the right-of-way to any bicycles in the opposite lane. Remember, they may be travelling more quickly than you expect.

A bicycle may turn left in two ways: from the same road position as a motor vehicle, or as a pedestrian, by dismounting

and walking the bicycle across the crosswalks.

Action: Give the same consideration for a left-turning bicycle as for any motor vehicle or pedestrian.

A bicycle can be difficult to see because of its small size, especially to the left and rear of your vehicle (your left blind spot).

Action: Be sure to look for bicycles, as well as cars, before you change lanes.

Turning right:

One of the most common car/bike collisions happens when a motor vehicle turns right at an intersection without seeing a bicycle to its right. It is particularly a problem when the lane is dual-purpose, where vehicles can turn right or go straight ahead, as bicyclists generally ride on the right side of the road.

Action: Always check behind and to your right (your right blind spot) before turning right. Stay behind bicyclists and allow them to continue through the intersection before making your turn.

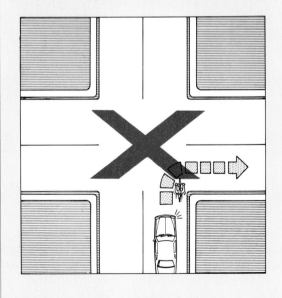

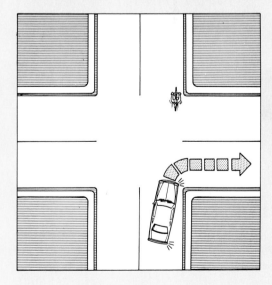

Bicycles at intersections:

Bicyclists may be approaching an intersection quickly and may be difficult to see. They may fail to stop at a stop sign or stop-signal, especially if they are children and are not aware of the total traffic situation. A common intersection accident happens when a motor vehicle hits a bicycle from the bicycle's left.

Action: Scan for bicycles, as well as cars, especially to your right.

A bicycle, like any other vehicle, has the right-of-way if it arrives first at a four-way stop.

Action: Yield the right-of-way to the bicycle, if it arrives first. Yield if you arrive at the same time and the bicycle is on your right.

At dusk, night, in rain, fog, or snow:

Even bicycles with proper lighting are difficult to see when it is dark, rainy, or foggy. In rain or snow, their braking distance is greatly increased.

Action: Look out for bicycles in these situations, especially in residential areas. Look for the up-and-down movement of pedal reflectors. Slow down when passing and be especially alert on rural roads, where nighttime accidents are most common. Allow for bicycles needing extra braking distance on wet roads.

Leaving a parked car:

Another common cause of car/bike collisions happens when a driver or a passenger opens a motor vehicle door in front of a bicycle.

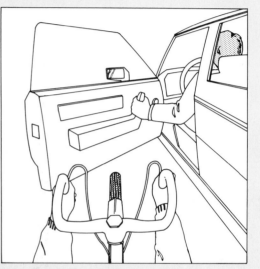

Action: Always look for bicycles before you open your door, on both the driver and passenger sides.

Special Areas

You can find off-street areas, one-way streets, school zones, and tunnels almost everywhere, but they are especially common in the city. You should become familiar with these special areas and learn how to drive through them safely.

Off-street areas

Off-street areas refer to parking lots, driveways, shopping plazas, and laneways. Cars are often coming from several directions at once. People are walking around and often aren't watching for cars.

Also, your line of sight may be blocked by parked cars or buildings. For all these reasons, you have to be extra careful and drive slowly.

In parking lots and shopping malls, try to follow the routes for traffic indicated by signs and pavement markings if there are any. You should not drive diagonally across an empty parking area. Drive slowly so you can stop quickly if you have to. Always yield the right-of-way to pedestrians. When moving out of an off-street area, you must yield the right-of-way to passing traffic.

One-way streets

Sometimes city traffic planners decide that for reasons of safety or to control traffic flow through a neighbourhood, a street should be made one-way. This means that traffic can travel in one direction only.

There are a number of special rules for one-way streets. For example, if you hear an emergency vehicle siren, the law normally requires you to pull over to the right. However, on a one-way street it is also permissible to pull over to the left if it is safe to do so.

Throughout this book the situations described normally refer to two-way traffic. However, wherever there are important differences for one-way streets, these will be explained.

Tunnels

Slow down and proceed with caution when you approach a tunnel. Even on a sunny day it is hard to see in tunnels. Generally it is safer to drive through them with your low beam headlights on (unless, of course, a sign tells you not to).

Because space is often limited in tunnels, you may not be able to keep a large space cushion to the sides. This means you

should leave an even greater gap between your car and the one ahead of you. This helps you avoid sudden braking which could lead to a rear-end collision.

School zones

M.T.C. Ont.

Drive especially carefully if there is a school in the area. A school zone is often indicated by a special sign and a reduced speed limit. At school crossings, you are required by law to stop for school crossing guards guiding children across the road. But remember to watch out for children crossing the street at other points, too. Small children often aren't aware of how dangerous traffic can be.

Unless prohibited by law, you should drive through tunnels with your low beam headlights on.

School buses

On highways, country roads, city, town, or village streets, regardless of the posted speed limit, motorists *meeting* a stopped school bus with red lights flashing and/or a stop arm extended must stop unless they are on a highway divided by a median strip.

Motorists travelling in the *same direction* behind a stopped school bus with red lights flashing and/or a stop arm extended on *any* type of road (highway, freeway, city street) must always stop before reaching the bus. In both cases,

motorists may not proceed until the bus resumes motion, or the lights have stopped flashing and the stop arm is retracted. In some provinces, the minimum distance you must leave between your car and the stopped school bus is specified by law.

Conviction for failure to stop when required carries a large fine for a first offence; a larger fine and accumulation of demerit points and a possible jail sentence for subsequent offences.

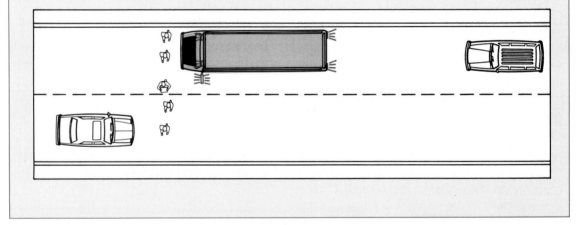

5

Driving on Highways and Country Roads

In this chapter you will learn:

- *how to pass and make other manoeuvres on undivided highways*
- *about the special features of country roads*
- *what to do at a railway crossing*
- *how to prevent head-on collisions*
- *how to plan a long trip*
- *how to drive with a heavy load and trailer*

Highways and Country Roads

So far in this unit you have learned about driving on city streets. You will now learn about the special skills needed for driving on highways and on country roads. In chapter 6, you will learn about driving on freeways.

Highways are high-speed roads on which oncoming traffic is separated from you by only a painted line down the centre of the road. These highways will probably also have sharp turns, railway crossings, signal lights and stop signs. In addition, they probably won't have wide, paved shoulders to rely on if you go off the road, but soft, sandy surfaces or ditches which may well prove hazardous. The high-speed country roads you travel on are likely to be made of gravel or dirt. You will have to deal with potholes and bumpy road surfaces.

You might think because there are fewer cars travelling on them that driving on highways and country roads is safer than travelling on freeways and city streets. But this is not true. In fact, the statistics show that there is more risk of serious traffic accidents in rural areas.

A major reason is that people tend to drive faster on country roads than the road conditions permit. And the faster you drive, the greater the risks you take. The chances of getting hurt or killed increase as the speed of your car increases. This is for several reasons:

1. The faster you go, the less time you will have to identify hazards and avoid them.

2. The faster you go, the less time other drivers have to react to you.

3. The faster you go, the greater the stopping distance for your car.

4. The faster you go, the greater the chances your car will skid on a turn or miss it altogether.

5. The faster you go, the greater the force of impact will be in a collision.

Increasing your speed does not save you very much time. When you also consider that even a little more speed makes a crash much more severe, it makes sense that you should slow down and travel at a speed suitable for the road conditions.

Highway Manoeuvres

Passing

When driving on a multi-lane freeway, you can avoid a slower-moving vehicle by making a simple lane change. However, highways and rural roads often have only one lane in each direction. And these lanes are usually only divided by painted centre lines. This means that to pass another car, you may have to cross left of the centre line into the lane of *oncoming* traffic.

There is always the risk of a head-on collision when you cross the centre line. For this reason you need to be extremely careful before making this driving manoeuvre.

First, you shouldn't pass if your view ahead is blocked or if space to pass is limited. Never pass on a curve, hill or bridge, at an intersection, or in a tunnel. All of these

make it difficult for a driver to see ahead, so collisions are more likely.

Second, don't pass if cars on side roads may pull out onto the main road. Avoid passing if cars ahead are grouped so tightly that you don't have space to re-enter the right lane.

Finally, don't pass if the car you want to overtake is moving close to the maximum speed. You will have to speed up in order to pass the car and return to the right lane. And this would mean you'd have to go over the speed limit.

To pass another car on a two-lane road, do the following:

1. Make sure it's advisable to pass on this section of roadway. If so, there will be a broken yellow line down the middle of the road as you can see from the diagrams on this page. Watch also for signs advising you it is unsafe to pass and obey them.

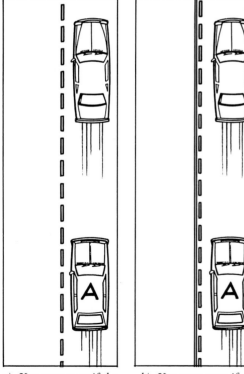

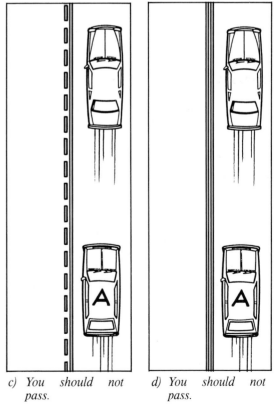

a) *You may pass if the road is clear ahead and behind.*

b) *You may pass if the road is clear ahead and behind.*

c) *You should not pass.*

d) *You should not pass.*

2. Don't get closer than the standard two-second following distance from the car you want to pass.

3. Check ahead for a safe passing gap. If you can see an oncoming car, you will need to judge whether or not it is a safe distance away.

4. Check rear-view mirrors and your left blind spot. Another driver behind you may be trying to pass at the same time.

5. If the oncoming lane ahead is clear, signal a left turn and check your mirror and blind spot again.

6. Accelerate into the oncoming lane. Keep looking well ahead into the distance.

7. Be prepared to drop back if the driver you are preparing to pass moves uncertainly or speeds up. Also be prepared to do so if you suddenly find your intended path blocked.

8. Signal a return to the right lane.

9. Pull into the right lane when you can see the entire front end of the passed car in your rear-view mirror.

10. Cancel your turn signal. Check the position of the passed car in your rear-view mirror. Make sure you are a safe distance ahead of the car you have passed before you slow down.

Before attempting to overtake another vehicle on an undivided highway, be sure you can see ahead clearly. Also make sure that the oncoming lane is free of traffic far into the distance. If you have any doubt whatsoever about passing safely, don't pass. Head-on collisions at highway speeds are almost always fatal.

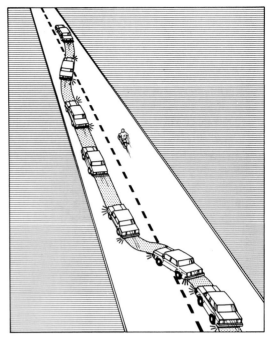

Passing On Two Lane Roads

Being passed

There are two important things you can do to prevent something dangerous from happening when you are being passed. When another driver is trying to pass you, move to the right side of your lane. This will give the passing driver more room and a better view of what's up ahead. And as the passing driver speeds up to overtake you, make sure you don't go faster yourself, but maintain a steady speed. This helps the passing driver to judge the speed and distance needed to pass safely.

Climbing and Passing Lanes

Many highways have specially constructed lanes called climbing or passing lanes. These lanes allow slower vehicles to move into the right-hand lane while faster vehicles pass safely in the left lane. Signs are posted well in advance of these lanes to inform drivers that they will soon have a chance to pass.

It is important to remember that at the end of the climbing or passing lane, drivers of vehicles in the right-hand lane will have to merge back into the centre lane of traffic. Drivers in the centre lane should always allow the slower vehicles in and not try to cut them off.

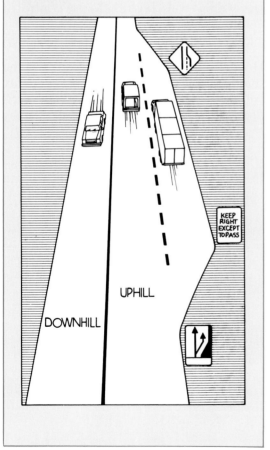

Steering on Highway Curves

Highway curves can create problems. For one thing, they limit how far a driver can see ahead. This means you may not be able to see trouble ahead until it's too late. Highway curves can also create problems because they may be very sharp. Momentum acts on your car when you go around a curve. It can cause your car to skid or miss the curve altogether. In fact, running off the road in a curve is one of the most common causes of serious accidents for young drivers, even for those with enough experience to know better.

The chances of skidding or leaving the road depend on three things: your car's speed, characteristics of the curve, and condition of the road.

Speed

As the speed of your car increases, the chances of skidding on a curve or going off the road also increase. In some cases, speed advisory signs are posted before curves on the highway. Such signs tell you the maximum safe speed at which to approach the curve. Think ahead so you don't have to brake while *in* the curve. Always reduce your speed *before* you enter it. As you are rounding the curve, maintain a constant speed. Accelerate gently out of the curve.

Characteristics of the curve

The sharper a curve, the more traction is needed to hold a car on the road at a given speed. Therefore, the sharper a curve is, the more you will have to slow down beforehand to negotiate the curve safely. Curves may be "banked" or tilted slightly to keep vehicles on the road.

You should look across any curve before you enter it. This will allow you to judge how much you have to slow down. While rounding a curve, remember to aim your eyes high and well ahead. Keep looking across the curve. This will help keep your steering smooth. Don't look along the hood of the car or at the road shoulder.

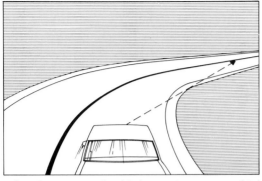

When driving, you should always aim your eyes high and well ahead, and look across curves as far ahead as you can see.

Road conditions

If the road is wet, icy, unpaved, or bumpy, you will have to slow down more than usual before going around a curve. Under such conditions, traction will be reduced a great deal.

Driving onto the Shoulder

The "shoulder" of a road is usually a fairly narrow, paved or unpaved, strip on the sides of some roadways. City streets seldom have shoulders. Freeways often have wide, paved shoulders. The shoulder of a highway or rural road is often made of dirt or gravel and separates the roadway from a rain ditch, fence, or field.

If you are alert and paying close attention to your driving, you should notice the road shoulder as you drive. Is it level with the roadway, or is there a drop? How wide is the shoulder? Is it paved or soft? Are there fixed objects such as a fence or telephone poles near it? Knowing the answers to these questions will prepare you for getting safely back on the road if your car drops off onto a soft shoulder.

Going onto the shoulder of a country highway is dangerous. It is easy to lose control of your car at high speeds, especially if there is a large drop from the road to the shoulder.

However, if your wheel does drop onto the shoulder, don't panic. If you react suddenly without thinking, you may have an accident. Also, don't slam on your brakes or try

If your vehicle goes onto the shoulder, slow down gradually and then steer back onto the road.

to steer back onto the pavement right away at a high speed. Do the following:

1. Grip the steering wheel firmly. Otherwise the car may pull even farther onto the shoulder.

2. Don't brake to a full stop. Slow down gradually by braking lightly. Don't try to get back onto the road immediately unless there is an obstacle on the shoulder just ahead. If you can, straddle the road and shoulder by keeping the left wheels of your car on the pavement.

3. When the car is under control at low speed, check your blind spots, turn the steering wheel sharply to the left to allow the front tire to climb up the edge of the pavement and back onto the roadway. If you don't steer sharply enough, your front wheel will scuff along the pavement edge.

4. Once the right front tire is back on the roadway, steer quickly to the right. It will help keep your car in the far right lane away from oncoming traffic.

You may find yourself in the dangerous position of having to return to the road very quickly after your car drops onto the shoulder. A quick return to the roadway will be needed if, for example, you are in danger of going into a ditch or an object is blocking the shoulder ahead.

In these situations, you won't have time to slow down. In order to get back onto the road, steer sharply to the left. When you feel the front tire hit the edge of the pavement, steer sharply to the right. This should prevent your car from shooting across the lane into the far lane on the other side of the road. At all times you need to keep a firm grip on the steering wheel so you don't lose control of the car. Having your seat belt fastened will also help keep you in your seat and in control.

Conditions on Country Roads

Road Surfaces

In rural areas you may drive on gravel roads or even find yourself on a trail road. You may also have to drive through sand or up steep hills. These different surfaces require different driving skills.

Gravel roads

Controlling your car can be difficult on gravel roads. Often they develop ridges which are known as "wash boards." They can make your car "fishtail" or swing from side to side unless you drive more slowly. Soft shoulders can also be a problem. They tend to pull a car off the road once one of the wheels has run onto the shoulder.

When you drive on a gravel road, the gravel and stones spin underneath the wheels of your car. This increases braking distance. It also means you will have to cope with dust and flying stones thrown up by the car ahead. Unless you stay well behind the car in front of you, you may find yourself with a damaged windshield or broken headlight.

It's always a good idea when you come to the end of a gravel road to check and see if there is any damage to your car, especially to the headlights and tires.

Trail roads

Trail roads are not heavily travelled and are usually located in remote areas. They tend to be used much more by trucks than by cars. For these reasons, trail roads are always unpaved and rugged.

If you find yourself on a trail road you will probably be faced with many obstacles. The road will be narrow and you'll come across sharp turns and short, steep hills. These features will reduce your ability to see ahead. If another car or truck appears, you will have little time for evasive action. As a precaution it's wise to stay as much as possible on your side of the road, keep your headlights on, and drive slowly.

You may also have to deal with water-filled potholes. Try to straddle them if you can. They might be deeper than you think. And even if they're not deep enough for you to get stuck in, you won't want wet brakes. If the road is just two tracks through the woods or bush, watch out for rocks or tree stumps sticking up in the centre. These obstacles may not be high enough to cause trucks any trouble, but could easily damage the bottom of a car. Drive over them very slowly, or go around them.

Muddy roads

Mud can be sticky or slippery and can form deep ruts. You're more likely to come across a muddy road after a rain storm or in swampy, marsh-like areas. Mud makes it difficult for your car's tires to grip the road because the road surface is uneven and the mud fills the tire grooves. However, if your tires are in good condition, it will be a little easier for them to grip the road. As with sand, be careful not to drive too fast, stop suddenly, or turn sharply on a muddy road. The faster you drive, the less traction your tires will have.

If you are stuck in deep mud or sand, put flat rocks, small tree branches, cardboard, or traction pads under the tires. This may give them better traction and help free the car. Even so, getting free may be hard because sand and mud don't pack down well.

Hilly roads

To go down a long, steep hill, shifting into low gear will help control your car's speed. You will also have to brake less. However, you should shift in advance since it may not be possible to downshift on the decline itself.

The greatest danger on hilly roads is your inability to see oncoming vehicles. If the road is narrow and relatively untravelled, drivers may drive in the centre of the road.

When travelling on a narrow, hilly road, keep well to the right to avoid oncoming vehicles which may be in the centre of the road.

This, of course, is an invitation to disaster. It will help prevent a head-on collision if you keep well to the right side and tap your horn lightly just before you reach the top of the hill.

Sometimes two cars going in opposite directions meet on a narrow, hilly road. It is common courtesy in this situation for the driver going downhill to slow down or stop and give way to the person going uphill. It will be much easier for the driver going downhill to get moving again than it would have been for the driver going uphill.

Mountain roads

Although you can see some spectacular scenery when driving in the mountains, the trip will put a strain on your car. Make sure it is in good condition before you leave. Going up and down steep mountain roads can cause your engine to lose power and overheat. Mountain driving can also be nerve-racking. The roads will be narrow and winding, so you will have to drive slowly.

Don't always try to go as fast as the car in front of you. The driver may live in the area and know the roads really well. Travel along at a speed that you feel comfortable and safe with. If cars start to bunch up behind you, pull over and let them pass. Finally, let your passengers do all the scenery watching. It's safer if you keep your eyes on the road.

Don't Be a Litter Bug

One of the reasons people drive out into the country or through hills and mountains is to enjoy the beautiful scenery. Responsible drivers appreciate the beauty of the landscape and don't litter. Littering is ugly. It pollutes. And it is illegal in many places.

Do your share in keeping the landscape clean. Keep cigarette butts in the ashtray. They can pollute and cause costly fires. Don't throw garbage out the window; keep it in a plastic bag until you get to a garbage can. If all drivers acted responsibly, we wouldn't have situations like the one pictured below.

Other Road Users

When you drive in the country, you may go a long way before you see another car. However, don't think the whole road is yours. More than half of all traffic accidents in the country involve another vehicle. Always stay alert for other traffic.

Trucks

Trucks use country roads frequently. One thing to remember about them is that they climb hills very slowly but may go down them very quickly. Never try to pass a truck when it is going down a steep hill. You would have to go much too fast in order to overtake it.

If a truck passes you, stay to the far right of your lane. You can expect to get a blast of air as it goes by, and will therefore have to make steering adjustments to stay on the road. When following trucks or trailers which block your view of the road ahead, you should leave more space. This will do more than allow you to see around the truck. Trucks and trailers have large blind spots. They may slow down suddenly without seeing you. Keeping a larger space cushion may help prevent an accident.

School buses

You must stop for a school bus that is stopped with its signals flashing.

Especially in the early morning and late afternoon, you will likely encounter school buses on country roads. Most school buses are a bright yellow. They are equipped with red signal lights which have either a warning such as "do not pass when signals flashing" or "stop on signal" painted in large letters on the rear. Some even have stop arms as in the photograph.

On rural roads which are not divided by a median strip, vehicles meeting or approaching a stopped school bus with red lights flashing and/or a stop arm extended must stop. Even after a school bus has started moving again, you should proceed with caution. There is always a chance that a child may suddenly run across the road directly into your path.

Slow-moving vehicles

M.T.C. Ont.

You may come across slow-moving vehicles such as tractors in the country. They may have a slow-moving vehicle sign (a bright orange triangle) on the back to warn you. Slow down behind these vehicles and pass only when it's safe. Remember, too,

84

that often you will come upon these vehicles over a hill. If you are speeding, you may not be able to stop in time to avoid a collision.

Animals

You may also have to deal with farm animals or wild animals on the road. For example, you may encounter a horse and rider out for exercise, or a stray cow or a deer that is dashing across the road.

Always slow down as you approach an animal so you don't frighten it. If you do frighten the animal, it may suddenly jump into your path. A frightened horse may also throw its rider. It is always wise to pay attention to animal crossing signs.

A collision with a large animal can be hazardous both to you and to the animal. If a small animal darts out in front of you, however, it is better to hit it, if you must, than to swerve and crash into a larger obstacle or to stop suddenly and risk a collision with the car behind you.

In construction zones obey all signs and any workers who are directing traffic through the area. Slow down and be prepared to stop.

Special Obstacles

Although you can find construction zones, bridges and railway crossings in the city as well, they are much more common in rural areas.

Construction zones

If there are workers repairing the road, slow down and be prepared to stop. Obey all construction signs and any workers who are directing traffic through the area. Be patient if traffic is delayed. Sometimes traffic in one direction must wait until several cars from the other lane pass through the detour. If your lane is blocked and no one is directing traffic, you must yield to the driver coming from the opposite direction. Let the other driver go through first. When the way is clear, move carefully around the obstruction. Go slowly.

Bridges

Slow down and proceed with caution when you approach a bridge. It may be difficult to manoeuvre your car because some bridges have narrow lanes. This makes head-on collisions more likely than on the open road. On very narrow country bridges it's often a good idea to wait and let an oncoming car cross over the bridge first before you proceed.

Railway crossings

There are two types of railway crossings— controlled and uncontrolled. At a *controlled* railway crossing, there will be a mechanical barrier or warning device to let you know if a train is coming. There are different rules for different types of controlled crossings. First, if there is a light signal, you must come to a full stop if it is flashing. When the light stops flashing, you can go if the track is clear. Second, if there is a crossing gate, you must come to a full stop when it is down. You are allowed to cross the tracks only after the gate is fully raised. Third, there may be a stop sign. Again, come to a full stop, look carefully in both directions, and go when the track is clear.

Never rely completely on the mechanical devices at controlled railway crossings. The devices may not be working properly and it's unwise to assume that they are. Always *look and listen* before you cross the tracks.

Often you will approach an *uncontrolled* railway crossing. At uncontrolled crossings, it is left up to the driver to decide when it is safe to cross. At an uncontrolled crossing, you should:

1. Slow down and look in both directions as you approach the crossing to see if there is a train coming.

2. Listen carefully for a train. (This requires turning off the radio and rolling down the window.)

3. If several cars are crossing, don't go until the car crossing in front of you is well past the tracks. Look both ways again and then cross with caution.

4. If there is more than one set of tracks, you should wait till any passing train is well down the tracks. This way you can make sure another train isn't coming from the opposite direction.

There are a few common sense rules to follow when approaching any railway crossing, whether controlled or uncontrolled. First, remember that in some areas, trucks carrying dangerous cargoes and buses are legally required to stop at some crossings whether or not there is a train coming. If you are behind one of these vehicles, be prepared to stop. Second, stop at least five metres back from the tracks if a train is coming. Third, never change gears while crossing railway tracks, and never stop on the tracks. What would you do if your car stalled and a train suddenly appeared? You only have seconds to make the right decision. Never try to beat a train. A collision with a train is usually fatal for the occupants of the car.

Operation Lifesaver
—"Beat the train" is a dangerous game

So you don't call yourself a gambler. You're an average citizen. Yet only yesterday, you and thousands of other Canadian drivers gambled with your lives in a game called "beat the train".

Railway companies and governmental agencies have long been concerned about the needless losses of life, the injuries and heavy material damages caused by highway/railroad crossing accidents and the need to reduce them. An ambitious and aggressive program to upgrade rail/highway crossings and install additional automatic warning devices was undertaken. However, despite these efforts, the number of people killed and injured has not decreased nearly as much as expected.

Too often motorists ignore the signs of life—disregard warning signals of an approaching train and even drive around the lowered crossing gates and past the flashing warning lights.

A recent survey disclosed that in 16% of the cases, the drivers of motor vehicles ignored the flashers and bell warning, that in 2% of the cases they drove around the lowered barriers, that in 6% of the cases they misjudged their safety margin, and finally, in 6% of the cases they ignored the train whistle and bell warnings.

The results of such research and surveys and the almost static number of rail/highway crossing accidents despite the addition of improved warning devices indicate that a lack of knowledge about rail/highway crossing hazards is a part of the problem and therefore, clearly a part of the solution. To deal with this problem, Operation Lifesaver was established.

A joint project of The Railway Association of Canada and of Transport Canada in co-operation with the Canada Safety Council, Operation Lifesaver's goal is to join all Provincial as well as Federal authorities in a nationwide effort to reduce deaths, injuries and property damages resulting from rail/highway crossing accidents.

Operation Lifesaver focuses on three areas of activity:

1. EDUCATION—the success of the operation consists in alerting people of all ages to the "high-risk" aspects of rail/highway crossings. This will be done through community presentations, elementary school and driver education curriculum activities, as well as media coverage.

2. ENFORCEMENT—Provincial and municipal law enforcement agencies will be urged to "crack down" on motorists and pedestrians who disregard the law and jeopardize their lives and the lives of others.

3. ENGINEERING—The public will be alerted to Federal and Provincial Government safety programs—and others—dealing with planning, construction and maintenance of rail/highway crossings.

Excerpted from *The Fleet Supervisor*, courtesy of the Ontario Safety League.

The Dangers of Rural Driving

Traffic Fatalities

Recent Canadian statistics show that there are three times more traffic accidents causing injury in urban areas than in rural areas. However, for traffic *deaths* the statistics are reversed. Over half of all fatal traffic accidents happen in the country, despite the fact that more people drive in urban areas than in rural areas.

There are four main reasons for these findings. First, there is less traffic in the country and in towns, so people often drive faster and less carefully than in cities. Higher speed means more serious injury in case of an accident. Second, many people driving in the country aren't familiar with rural roads. Third, because there are more uncontrolled intersections and fewer safety features such as wide lanes and median strips, head-on collisions are more likely to occur. And finally, the nearest doctor or hospital can be many kilometres away in the country. Delays in getting emergency medical care can result in a more serious injury or death through loss of blood or shock.

Preventing Head-On Collisions

You can help reduce the high death rate by driving carefully. There are a number of things you can do as a responsible driver to lower the risk to yourself, your passengers, and other road users.

Know what to look for

When a car crosses over the centre line of a highway or road, that car is a hazard to other drivers who are coming towards it. It helps to know why a driver might move into the oncoming lane. This will help you identify signs of danger in advance and, hopefully, avoid a head-on collision. A car might swerve into your lane for one of the following reasons:

1. **Driving manoeuvres**. Overtaking, making a left turn, and going around a curve are examples of driving manoeuvres which may put a car in your path.
2. **Reduced space**. Parked cars, snowdrifts, narrow bridges, and other situations may force an oncoming car to move into your lane.
3. **Poor visibility**. Bright sunlight, glaring headlights, snow, rain, fog, or darkness may prevent a driver from seeing exactly where he or she is on the road and what is ahead.
4. **Loss of control**. A driver may lose control of a car because of poor road conditions, a skid, or a tire blowout. Or the driver may lose control because he or she is impaired.

Besides these general conditions, there are specific driving situations where a head-on crash is more likely. You should always be alert for these situations. For example:

1. **Meeting an oncoming line of cars**. Whenever you meet a long line of cars, you can be sure there will always be one driver who is anxious to get ahead of the rest. Often this driver will not look before he or she tries to pass. As a responsible driver you should let the impatient driver know you are there. Turn on your headlights so your car will be seen more easily. Also, drive closer to the right side of the road. This will put extra space between your car and the oncoming ones.
2. **Meeting on curves and hilltops**. Winding and hilly roads restrict how far ahead you can see. At night your headlights will let other drivers know you are approaching. When you do meet a vehicle travelling in the opposite direction, slow down and move as close to the right side of the road as possible.

3. Meeting at night. At night on lonely country roads you should use your high beam headlights. However, these can blind the driver in an oncoming car. Therefore you should always switch to low beam if you see another car approaching. As you meet and pass, look ahead and slightly to the right of the centre of the road in order to avoid being blinded yourself by the other driver's headlights.

Lower the risk

If a collision seems unavoidable, there are ways to reduce the seriousness of the crash. Above all, don't freeze. *Keep trying*. The chances are you will be hurt less if you stay calm and are prepared to react quickly and correctly. The first thing you should do is to *slow down*. The more slowly you are going, the lower the force of impact will be. A small reduction in speed leads to a big reduction in the force of a crash. Slowing down also increases the space between your car and the approaching vehicle. You will have more time and room to manoeuvre your car out of danger.

Second, *move to the right if you can*. Moving to the left would put you in danger of colliding both with other oncoming traffic and with the driver of the approaching vehicle if he or she manages to recover at the last moment. If necessary, steer off the road towards something soft that will "give" or bend when your car hits it. For example, it is better to plow into some bushes or a chain metal fence than into a big tree. If you don't have enough time to do this, it is better to sideswipe the oncoming vehicle than hit it head-on. Alert the oncoming driver by sounding your horn. Try to slow down as much as you can and steer to the right.

These evasive manoeuvres may well save your life. They can be even more effective if you think ahead. As you drive, identify what things are potential hazards and plan your escape routes in advance. However, there is one thing that you should never have to think about in an emergency: seat belts. If you and your passengers are not already wearing them, it will be too late.

Hitch-Hiking

On any long journey you are bound to encounter hitch-hikers. You may feel sympathetic and want to help them out. However, there are some things you should consider very carefully before offering a stranger a lift.

First of all, just stopping your car to pick up a hitch-hiker can be dangerous. If you suddenly pull over to the side you risk a rear-end collision. Rejoining traffic which is travelling at highway speeds can be a difficult and hazardous manoeuvre.

Second, think about whether you can trust a hitch-hiker. Certainly some hitch-hikers are honest, friendly individuals in need of help. However, many are dishonest and even dangerous. Drivers who have generously offered hitch-hikers a lift have sometimes found themselves robbed. Some have even been beaten or killed. No matter whether you are male or female, you should be extremely cautious about picking up strangers.

When you think about it, hitch-hikers are running a grave risk too. How can they be sure the driver who picks them up won't rob *them*? And how can they be sure he or she is a responsible driver? All things taken into consideration, hitch-hiking is a dangerous practice which should be avoided.

Taking a Long Trip

Preparing for the Journey

Canadians often drive in the country while they are on holiday. Part of going on a holiday is planning your trip. There will be maps to check, budgets to figure out, and maintenance checks on your car to do. This may take a bit of effort but it will be well worth it. A vacation is no time to worry whether your car will get you home.

Decide on a route

Before you leave you should know the exact route you expect to take. Do you want to stay on the fast, main highways or is a quiet, scenic drive more what you have in mind? Whatever the case, you will need to be sure there will be service stations and places to eat and sleep along the way.

This information is given on road maps which are available from most service stations, travel clubs, and tourist information booths. The maps will tell you how far it is between towns and cities. They may also show where hospitals, golf courses, airports, and tourist attractions can be found.

To read a map, you'll first have to look at the legend in the corner. It will tell you what the symbols on the map mean. There will also be a scale for estimating distance, and an alphabetical index of city names. To locate a city or a town on the map, look up the name of the city on the index. Beside the name of the city, there will be a letter and a number. Find where the letter and number are on the edges of the map. With one finger starting on the letter and one on the number, move your fingers down and across in straight lines. You will find the city located somewhere near where your fingers meet.

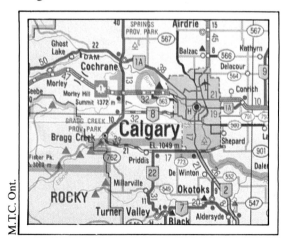

M.T.C. Ont.

It is best to plan each day's route in advance. This way you won't have to keep stopping to look at the map. Instead you can concentrate on driving and enjoying the countryside. It is also a good idea to take a felt-tip pen and mark your route clearly. Passengers will then find it easier to help you with directions.

Never try to look at a map and drive at the same time: you could easily cause an accident. Pull off the road in order to study your map. And if you do get lost, don't just drive around hoping to find your way again: you'll only waste time and fuel. Find a service station or store and ask for directions.

Check your car

An unexpected mechanical failure can ruin your vacation. Therefore it is recommended that your car be given a complete checkup by a professional mechanic, especially if your trip will be a long one. As you can see in the illustration on this page, there are also a number of simple checks you should do yourself or have done by your local service station attendant.

Check your documents

In a number of provinces there are some documents you should never travel without. You must carry with you your driver's licence and your vehicle permit and insurance certificate.

It is also always advisable to leave details about your route or destination with a relative, friend, or neighbour. Your journey may take you into remote areas of the country, or there may be dangerous storms in an area you expect to travel through. Or relatives at home may need to contact you about an urgent family matter. In all cases the authorities will find it easier to locate you or see that you are safe if you've left details of your journey with someone at home.

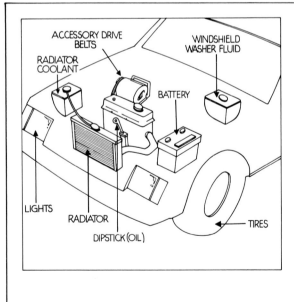

Checks to make before taking a trip:
1. *Make sure the tires are in good condition and have enough air in them. Check the spare tire too. Increase the tire pressure if travelling with a heavy load.*
2. *Check all the lights—including headlights, brake lights, tail lights, directional signals, and hazard signals.*
3. *Fill up the windshield washer fluid bottle and check that the wiper blades are in good condition.*
4. *Check the oil level and have it changed if necessary.*
5. *Check the accessory drive belts and tighten if necessary.*
6. *Make sure there is enough coolant in the radiator coolant tank.*
7. *Check the water level in the battery.*
8. *Clean the car windows inside and outside.*

The Trans-Canada Highway

M.T.C. Ont.

Lake Superior near Thunder Bay, Ontario

L.P. Lonero

Ferry from North Vancouver, British Columbia

In 1949, the federal and provincial governments entered into a cost-sharing agreement to construct a 7 850 km paved highway across Canada. This involved linking existing highways of good quality with highways that required upgrading, and constructing new connecting links where needed. On September 3, 1962, the Trans-Canada Highway was officially opened.

Signal Hill, St. John's, Newfoundland

West of Calgary, Alberta

St. John River near Woodstock, New Brunswick

Loading Your Car

On a long journey you're bound to be carrying a lot of luggage. And any heavy weight poorly distributed in the car can make steering difficult. Packing your car properly can take a bit of work and rearranging. However, putting things in their right place before you leave will ensure a much safer trip. When you pack your car, keep the weight low and centred. This will give you better handling of the car.

All heavy items belong in the trunk. Try to fit everything in snugly so nothing rattles around. If anything sticks out from the back of the trunk, tie a red flag to the article as a warning. You should not carry anything that sticks out on either side of the car. Tie down the lid of the trunk securely with a rope.

Do not put large, heavy objects on the passenger seats. Also, don't put anything on the dashboard or back ledge. If you have to stop quickly, these items are sure to fly off and hit someone. They also block your view out the windows. If you have to keep something inside the car, place it on the floor in the back.

If you use a roof rack, get one that can be securely attached to the top of the car. Having weight on the roof of your car changes the car's centre of gravity. This will make the car lean more when you go around curves and corners. Also, things can fall off the roof rack and easily cause an accident. Each time you stop, check to make sure nothing has come loose.

Towing a Trailer

Driving a car with a trailer has its own legal responsibilities and requires added driving skills. Each province has its own set of laws about trailers. It's best to know them before you leave.

If you are pulling a trailer, it will have to be carefully packed. Sixty percent of the total weight of the load should be in the front half of the trailer. The back of your car will have to support part of the trailer's weight, so don't overload the trunk of the car. You'll find that your car handles differently with the extra weight. This is one reason why you will have to increase the pressure in your car's tires. Check the car owner's manual for details. It is not safe to travel with passengers in the trailer, and it may be illegal.

You will need more manoeuvring room for making turns, so start from a position that is slightly farther away from the curb. Going uphill will be harder because of the added weight of the trailer so you may need to use a lower gear.

Backing with a trailer is probably the most difficult driving manoeuvre to accomplish. To back, turn the steering wheel in the opposite direction to the one in which you want the trailer to move. If you want to back the trailer to the right, steer to the left. You'll have to turn the steering wheel slowly and a small amount each time. Don't steer too sharply when backing because the car and trailer may "jackknife."

Manoeuvring with a trailer may be difficult. For this reason new drivers should wait until they have gained more driving experience before attempting to pull a trailer.

6

Driving on the Freeway

In this chapter you will learn:

- *what makes freeways different*
- *how to enter a freeway*
- *the basic principles of freeway driving*
- *how to leave a freeway*
- *how to handle emergencies on a freeway*

Characteristics of Freeways

Driving on a freeway is quite different from driving on city streets or country roads and highways. Freeways, or "expressways" as they are sometimes called, are very different from other roads. As their name shows, they are specially designed to move vehicles quickly and efficiently on heavily-travelled routes. For this reason you won't find any traffic lights or stop signs on freeways. And you'll also notice that there are special overpasses (or underpasses) for roads that cross their path.

Because they carry a lot of traffic, freeways are usually wide, well-paved roads marked into several lanes. They also have built-in safety features. Normally there is a median strip with or without a barrier that separates travel in two directions. There are no sharp turns, just gentle curves and hills. And the freeways have "controlled access"; there are special ramps to let vehicles on and off.

Entering a Freeway

How to Enter

There are usually two parts to a freeway entrance:

1. an entrance ramp, and
2. an acceleration lane.

The entrance ramp normally connects a lower-speed street to the higher-speed freeway. The acceleration lane allows the driver to accelerate up to the common speed of traffic. The driver then has to merge to enter the flow of freeway traffic.

To enter a freeway, do the following:

1. As you enter the entrance ramp, look for speed advisory signs. Entrance ramps can be sharply curved, so don't go over this speed. Otherwise you may have problems controlling your car or seeing far enough ahead.

2. As you move along the entrance ramp, look all around. Check for cars

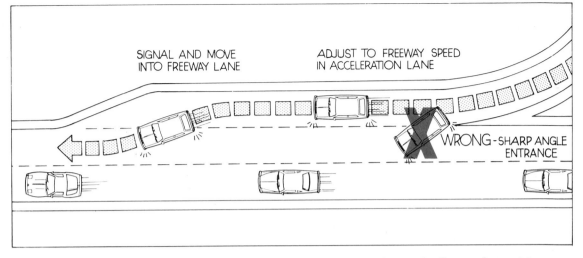

SIGNAL AND MOVE
INTO FREEWAY LANE

ADJUST TO FREEWAY SPEED
IN ACCELERATION LANE

WRONG - SHARP ANGLE
ENTRANCE

in front and behind and try to keep enough distance from them. Also, look at the traffic on the nearest freeway lane for a gap to enter. Are the cars spaced well apart or moving tightly together?

3. Before you reach the acceleration lane, turn on your directional signal. Keep checking for a space gap in the traffic flow by looking in your mirrors and glancing over your shoulder.

4. Once you are in the acceleration lane, start to increase speed. Make sure there is a big enough space gap in the freeway lane for you to enter safely. Then accelerate up to the common speed of traffic. This will allow you to merge safely with the traffic flow. If the acceleration lane is very short, it may be necessary to enter the flow of traffic at a speed lower than the common speed.

5. Once you are in the flow of traffic, turn off your directional signal and adjust your speed as necessary. Establish a space cushion around your car. Don't change lanes until you get used to the traffic and higher speed.

One very important thing to remember about entering a freeway is to always keep

an eye on the car in front of you. You may rear-end the car ahead while you are looking for a gap.

Always allow yourself enough distance from the car ahead to accelerate to the common speed before you merge with the stream of traffic. You should also think about the drivers behind you. It can be very dangerous to slow down once you are in the acceleration lane. You'll slow down everyone else behind you. You'll also enter high-speed traffic at a low speed and be in danger of being rear- ended yourself.

Entering a freeway in busy rush hour traffic requires constant scanning of the traffic flow and proper speed adjustment so that a merge can be made smoothly.

97

How to Handle Entrance Problems

Entering a freeway can be an unnerving experience, especially if you are a new driver. However, with practice you will find that it's not too difficult. The following are common problems you may have when entering a freeway, and ways to deal with them.

1. **You can't find a gap.** During rush-hour it may be very difficult to find a gap in the traffic flow. If traffic is too close together for you to merge safely, slow down at *the beginning of the acceleration lane* and proceed carefully. When you see a gap, start accelerating rapidly, make sure your directional signal is on, and merge with the traffic flow. *Never* stop at the end of the acceleration lane. You won't have enough space to accelerate to the common speed.

2. **There is an uncertain driver ahead.** Some drivers get very panicky when they have to enter fast-moving traffic. The best thing to do is to increase the space cushion between you and the car ahead. Give the other driver a bit of extra time to find a gap. Make sure the driver has merged with the traffic flow before you start to accelerate.

Above all, don't rush the other driver into making a mistake.

3. **There is a "weaving area."** In a weaving area cars that are exiting must cross the paths of other cars that are entering. Entering and exiting drivers should cooperate. Either slow down to let the other vehicle cross in front, or speed up to let it cross behind.

4. **The acceleration lane merges into the farthest left lane of traffic.** In this situation the fastest cars will be in the lane you enter first. You will have to accelerate even faster and make your decisions more quickly. Luckily, this type of acceleration lane is quite rare.

5. **You find yourself on the wrong entrance ramp.** Sometimes drivers find they have not been paying close enough attention to the signs and they have entered the wrong ramp. If you make a mistake, *don't back up*. Enter the freeway anyway and turn off at the next exit.

If you enter an *exit* ramp by mistake, you will meet oncoming traffic head on. This must be avoided at all costs. Pay close attention to all signs to be sure you are entering the proper entrance ramp.

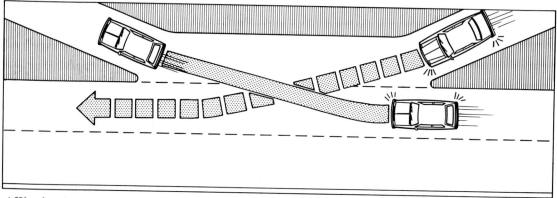

A Weaving Area

Driving Along on a Freeway

The principles of strategic driving described in Chapter 4 apply to freeway and highway driving as much as they do to city driving. But because speed limits on freeways and highways are so much higher than on city streets, you will also have to take into account the problems that come with travelling at faster speeds.

Strategic Driving

Looking

As in city driving, your eyes should be constantly moving, scanning the road ahead, to the sides, and behind. Be especially sure to *look into the distance* when you drive. When you travel at fast speeds, things in the distance come closer a lot faster. Concentrate on a distance of about fifteen to twenty seconds ahead of your car. At the same time, however, you need to be aware of what the drivers immediately ahead of you are doing, as well as what is going on in the distance far ahead.

You should also *remember to keep scanning*. The faster your car is moving, the worse your side vision becomes. Everything to the sides becomes blurred. Therefore your eyes tend to focus straight ahead where it's easier to see. Your field of vision becomes very narrow. To improve this, glance frequently to either side of your car where other vehicles can creep up unexpectedly.

Finally you should *check your rear-view mirrors frequently*. You need to know who's behind you, especially if they are tailgaters.

Maintaining a space cushion

It is especially important in freeway and highway driving to keep a large space cushion around your car. Remember to keep a space to your right and left on a freeway by not driving alongside other vehicles whenever possible. This will let you change lanes in an emergency such as if one of your tires blows out or the cars ahead come to a sudden stop.

It can also be quite dangerous travelling near large vehicles on high speed roads. Because of their large size, they block your vision more than other vehicles. Because they are so much heavier, they take longer to slow down and greater distance to make lane changes. You should therefore increase your space cushion when near large vehicles. Also, you should be careful not to cut off these vehicles when making a lane change.

In addition, large vehicles can affect your control of your car quite strongly and abruptly. For example, you may be driving along with a slight pressure on your steering wheel to the right in order to correct for a steady wind blowing from that direction. If you pass by a truck on your right, it will have the effect of blocking the wind. You may find yourself steering into the truck's path if you don't correct your steering quickly.

Communicating

Unlike the city where there is traffic coming from all directions and pedestrians and bicyclists to consider as well, on *freeways* there are no pedestrians or intersecting roads. Nevertheless even though the situation seems far less complicated, you still need to communicate with the other drivers.

First and most important, you should always signal and make a shoulder check before you change lanes. It's normally a good idea to avoid changing lanes if possible. However, if you must do so, you should always make sure the other drivers are aware of what you are doing. For example, it can be a dangerous situation if two drivers decide to move into the same spot in the lane between them. This can normally be avoided if you signal well in advance and try not to move into a lane right beside another car in case it moves over.

When changing lanes on multi-lane freeways, signal and shoulder check to be sure that another vehicle is not intending to move into the same lane as you.

Other drivers on the freeway won't expect you to slow down. If you do have to slow down because of trouble up ahead, signal as soon as possible. Tap your brake lights or put on your emergency flashers. Let drivers behind know your intentions right away.

You will also need to pay attention to the signals given to you by other drivers. In addition, when you drive on the freeway, there will be lots of signs to look at. These signs give important information. At high speeds, signs can pass by very quickly. Keep a careful watch into the distance. If you're not careful, you might end up on an exit ramp when you don't want to exit! Learn to identify different types of signs by their shape and colour. This way you will be able to recognize them faster.

High-Speed Driving

Legal speed limits are higher on freeways and highways than in the city. However, *maximum speed limits* are for good driving conditions only. You will need to slow down if the road surface, weather, or visibility is poor.

Freeways and highways in some areas also have *minimum speed limits* for good driving conditions. If you want to travel less than the minimum speed, travel on a different type of road. Even if there isn't a posted minimum speed limit, it is unwise, impolite, and often illegal to drive so slowly that you obstruct the flow of freeway or highway traffic. When other cars are travelling fast, a slow car can be a hazard.

Usually the safest speed (if it is within the posted speed limit) is the *common speed*. Travelling at the common speed helps your car blend in with the traffic around you. You won't have to speed up, slow down, or pass other vehicles as often. It also saves fuel.

Remember that differences in speed are a common cause of freeway and highway accidents. When you go faster than the rest of traffic, you will have to do a lot of unnecessary lane-changing and passing. This can be dangerous. The same is true if you drive too slowly. Other drivers may take risks in order to get past you.

Driving in the appropriate lane

Generally speaking, traffic in the left lanes of a *freeway* travels faster than traffic in the right. For this reason as a new driver you might want to drive in the right lanes until you become more confident driving at high speeds. You should never drive in the far left lane of a multi-lane freeway except to pass traffic moving at a rate below the speed limit.

On the freeway you should drive in the right-hand lane. If you wish to pass, pull into the passing lane, complete your pass, and return to the right-hand lane. If you are driving in the centre lane, keep checking your rear-view mirror. If there is a vehicle approaching from the rear, pull into the right-hand lane as soon as it is safe to do so and allow the vehicle to pass.

At every opportunity, do all you can to help faster traffic go through. It is an offence to block overtaking traffic by driving in the passing lane. And remember, on most freeways with three or more lanes in each direction, truck operators are prohibited from travelling in the left-hand passing lane. Therefore, they must use the centre lane for passing. So, it's much appreciated by the truck operators if you don't make a practice of driving in the centre lane.

Tailgaters

A common freeway problem is tailgating. Being a tailgater has no advantages. Tailgaters probably won't get to where they are going any faster and they might even have an accident along the way. In fact, tailgating has several real disadvantages. The closer tailgaters are to the car ahead:

- the less distance they can see ahead

- the more sharply they must steer in order to pass another car

- the more difficult it is to change lanes

- the less chance they will have to swerve around the car ahead if it stops suddenly

- the less chance they will have of braking in time to avoid hitting the car ahead if it stops suddenly.

As you can see, tailgating is dangerous. If someone is tailgating you, you won't have a safe space cushion behind your car. The problem is how to get that tailgater away. Try changing lanes, if you can do so safely. Sometimes you can slow down and move slightly to the right of the lane to encourage the tailgater to pass you. If the tailgater is still "glued" to your bumper, pull off the road at the next exit. It's too dangerous to be followed so closely at freeway speeds.

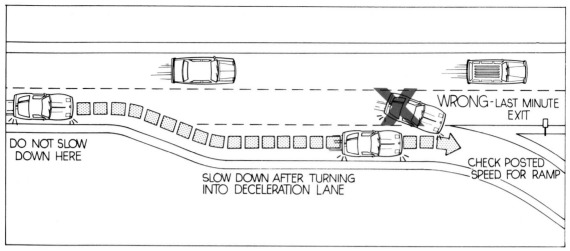

DO NOT SLOW DOWN HERE

SLOW DOWN AFTER TURNING INTO DECELERATION LANE

WRONG-LAST MINUTE EXIT

CHECK POSTED SPEED FOR RAMP

Exiting From a Freeway

How to Exit

There are usually three parts to a freeway exit:

1. a deceleration lane,
2. an exit ramp, and
3. a junction point.

The deceleration lane is an extra lane for exiting cars. It leads them out of the main flow of traffic so they can slow down safely. The exit ramp connects the freeway to a lower-speed roadway. The junction point is a stop or yield sign or traffic signal that allows drivers to join lower-speed traffic safely.

To leave a freeway, do the following:

1. About 500 metres before your exit, signal and prepare to move into the deceleration lane. However, do not start to slow down until you are in the deceleration lane itself.
2. Once you are in the deceleration lane, slow down gradually to the speed shown on the speed advisory signs. Adjust your speed and steering to suit the curve. Look as far ahead around the curve as you possibly can. Be cautious. Often you don't realize how fast you are really going because you've been used to the fast freeway speeds. Check your speedometer.
3. Be prepared to stop at the end of the exit ramp. There will usually be a stop sign or traffic light. Watch out for other traffic.

You should always anticipate your exit in advance. Watch for exit signs as you drive along the freeway. They will tell you how much farther you have to go before you reach your exit.

And if you are driving on a freeway in new territory, know in advance the exact name of the exit you will be using. Let's say that you are looking for the "King Street" exit. Unfortunately, the sign might not say "King Street." It might say "Highway 12 North" or "Business District" or "Exit 42" or something else. In short, study a map before you set out on your trip and be prepared.

How to Handle Exit Problems

Most of the time it is a little easier to get off a freeway than it is to get on one. Nevertheless, you are bound to encounter problems at some point. The following explains the most common problems in exiting from a freeway and how to deal with them.

1. **You don't notice your exit until the last minute**. If you miss the sign for your turn-off, or see your exit at the last moment, don't panic and make mistakes. If you miss your exit, you *must* go on to the next. Then take backstreets to your destination or get back on the freeway to reach the exit you want.

2. **The exit ramp you want is jammed with cars backed up onto the freeway**. In this situation, you have two choices. First, you can continue on and get off at the next exit. Or you can get in line with the other exiting cars and wait. If you do decide to get in line, signal early so drivers behind you know you're slowing down. Pump your brakes lightly so your brake lights flash on and off to warn drivers behind you of your intentions.

3. **There is a "weaving lane."** Weaving lanes are just as dangerous for drivers exiting from the freeway as they are for drivers trying to enter. Again, you will have to use your judgment in each situation. You will need either to slow down or speed up so as to allow entering drivers to get on to the freeway while you get off it.

Freeway Emergencies

Rear-End Collisions

There are many rear-end collisions on freeways, and these are far more dangerous than collisions on city streets. At high speeds, accidents are much more serious because of the greater force of the collision. The force of a car hitting something is called "force of impact." Force of impact builds up as the square of the speed of the car. This means for example that a car going 80 km/h will hit an object *four times* harder than at 40 km/h. Therefore, the impact felt by passengers in a car going 80 km/h will be *four times* greater than it would be in a 40 km/h crash.

This explains why passengers and drivers are killed more frequently in high speed crashes. A little more speed is a lot more dangerous! So don't forget to buckle up as you get in a car, either as the driver or as a passenger. Whether you are travelling on a multi- lane freeway or on a quiet street, that seat belt can save your life.

Rear-end collisions are most likely to occur near freeway exits. There are two common causes for these collisions. First, drivers sometimes try foolishly to exit at the last minute without signalling. Second, drivers sometimes suffer from "velocitization." This is loss of the ability to judge your speed accurately on a freeway or highway, causing you to travel faster than you think you are going. Velocitization is a special danger when leaving a freeway. You may misjudge your speed on the exit ramp and come suddenly upon traffic stopped at a junction point connecting a lower speed roadway. It is very important to be aware of your speed when exiting, and to slow down enough. Many drivers forget to do this and collisions are common.

The best way to avoid a rear-end collision is to stay alert and keep a safe following distance. You can prevent one by always keeping a space cushion to the sides, to the front, and to the rear of your car. By maintaining space to the sides, you have another choice besides braking to avoid a collision. Usually you can change lanes in less distance than it would take to stop.

Also, make sure to keep a following distance of a *minimum* of two seconds between your car and the car ahead. If someone cuts in front of you, don't get angry. Just slow down and make another space cushion. A responsible driver never forces a confrontation. Frequently check the tail lights of the car ahead, but don't keep your eyes on its bumper. Look past and through the car ahead. Be ready for the unexpected by constantly scanning around you. Know what signs of trouble to look for and how to deal with them. For example:

1. The brake lights of the car ahead come on. React right away by taking your foot off the accelerator or braking gently.

2. The spaces between cars ahead start to shrink. Increase your following distance by slowing down.

3. The rear bumper of the car ahead suddenly kicks up. The driver must have slammed on the brakes even though his or her brake lights are not working. Slow down and move into another lane if you can.

Usually the driver following is considered at fault in a rear-end collision. However, you can still do your share to avoid getting hit from behind. For example, you can:

1. Communicate early. If you intend to slow down, warn following drivers well in advance. Flash your brake lights. If you plan to change lanes, signal that intention early too.

2. Remember to maintain a space cushion around your car.

3. Always slow down gradually if you can. Don't brake suddenly.

4. Before changing lanes, look over your shoulder. There may be a driver in your blind spot. You may never see the car if you just rely on your mirrors.

5. Always think ahead. Be ready to react quickly and correctly if an emergency does arise.

Breakdowns

Being stuck on a freeway with fast-moving traffic whizzing by is no fun. Your car can break down due to mechanical failure when you least expect it. Know what to do in case it does.

Stop the right way

At the first sign of mechanical trouble with your car, put on your hazard warning signals. If possible, don't slow down until you've given advance notice to the drivers behind you. Move over towards the shoulder of the road as soon as you safely can. If you are in the passing lane, this will take more than one lane change.

If the shoulder is not paved, be prepared to make some steering adjustments, as your car may be difficult to control. Once you are on the shoulder, move as far away from the passing traffic as you can. Come to a full stop. If possible, get everyone out of the car and wait well away from it in a safe place off the road. If this is not possible, stay in your car. *Never* try to run or walk across freeway lanes.

Warn others

Even when you are safely off the road, it is important to warn other drivers that you are stopped. To alert other drivers, you should:

— leave on your hazard warning signals,

— tie a white cloth to the driver's door handle or the car's radio antenna, and

— raise the hood of the car.

At night, draw extra attention to your car by putting on the inside dome light or by lighting flares.

Wait for help

On a freeway, it's best to wait for help to arrive. Most freeways are patrolled regularly by police so you shouldn't have too long a wait. It's very dangerous to walk along a busy freeway, especially at night.

Never try to flag down motorists to help you. This can be very dangerous to both you and the helping driver. At freeway speeds, he or she will not have time to leave the road safely to help you. And whatever you do, don't try to get your car started again by having another car push it. There's a good chance you will get hit from behind by fast-moving traffic. Also, you can't push start modern cars with automatic transmissions anyway.

UNIT III

At Your Peril

7   Driving at Night and in Bad Weather

In this chapter you will learn:

- *how to drive safely at night*
- *how to drive in rainy weather*
- *how to handle winter driving problems*
- *how to drive on slippery and wet roads*
- *how to control skids*

Adapting to Poor Driving Conditions

The information we have given so far is for daytime driving under clear skies and at moderate temperatures. Unfortunately, drivers don't always experience such ideal conditions. Driving at night, for example, is less safe than driving during the day because it is harder to see. When the sun goes down, you have to rely on headlights, street lamps, and roadside reflectors to help you find your way. However, they allow you to see only a fraction of what you can normally see during daylight hours. Similarly, driving in rainy weather or in winter can be hazardous. A major problem is the loss of traction. Braking on a wet or icy road can result in a skid instead of a stop unless the correct braking technique is used.

There are two basic pieces of advice that will help you through these situations and any others caused by poor driving conditions. First *increase your space cushion* all around your car. On wet, snow-covered, or icy roads you can't be sure other drivers will be able to stop or change direction fast enough to avoid hitting your car. You, too, may need extra space to manoeuvre or stop on a slippery road. Second, *manoeuvre your car smoothly*. Any type of bad weather means you should do everything smoothly. This includes steering, accelerating, and braking. If you make any sudden change in speed or direction, your car may go into a skid. On slippery roads, steer your car gradually, accelerate very gently, and always leave yourself greater braking distance.

Of course, there are many more special precautions you can take in dealing with poor road conditions. This chapter will help you recognize the potential hazards of driving in the dark and in bad weather. It will explain how to avoid these hazards and how to deal with problems if they do arise.

Driving at Night

Even on a clear night, you cannot see most things as well as in the daytime. The only exception to this is seeing other cars. Often their headlights allow you to see cars sooner than you would have during the day. Nevertheless, it is harder to judge their speed and distance at night. And curves are more difficult to see in advance because you can only see as far as your headlights shine. You need to learn how to use your headlights and the lights of other drivers effectively, as well as how to accomplish common manoeuvres safely in the dark.

Headlights

Under ideal conditions, low beams light the road for about 45 m ahead of your car. High beams illuminate the road for about 135 m ahead. Unfortunately in true driving situations, these distances are often reduced. Incorrectly aimed headlights do not light the road as effectively. Dirty headlights do not produce as much light. And dirty windshields and glasses cut down on the amount of light getting to your eyes. Finally, the headlights of oncoming cars cause glare and reduce the distance you can see with your own lights.

Over-driving your headlights

Over-driving is driving so fast that your stopping distance is greater than the distance your headlights allow you to see. Imagine, for example, you are travelling on a dry road at 80 km/h and need 60 m to stop your car. If you are driving with your low beam lights on, you can only see approximately 45 m ahead. This means that once your headlights spot something in the road 45 m ahead, you won't be able to stop in time. You would be *over-driving* your low beam headlights by approximately 15 m. But if you reduce your speed to 70 km/h and spot something in the road

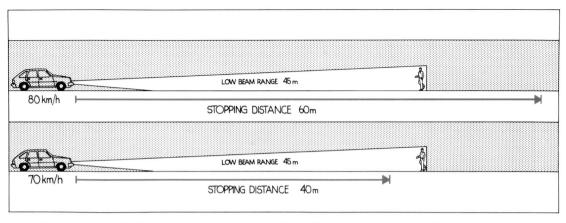

LOW BEAM RANGE 45 m

80 km/h

STOPPING DISTANCE 60m

LOW BEAM RANGE 45 m

70 km/h

STOPPING DISTANCE 40m

Over-driving your headlights occurs when you are driving so fast that your stopping distance is greater than the distance your headlights allow you to see. So slow down at night, especially on unlit highways and country roads.

45 metres ahead, you will only need 40 m to stop your car and should be able to avoid hitting the object.

One of the major problems in driving at night is seeing objects that do not have lights on them. Road signs are an exception. They have been made with special reflective coatings. For this reason, road signs are visible in your headlights at a much greater distance than other unlighted objects. It is important for these signs to be visible from as great a distance as possible. But this visibility has an important and dangerous side effect.

Your judgment of the distance your headlights let you see is affected by the extra visibility of signs. You can see reflectorized signs in your high beams when you are still 200 to 300 metres away. That's 2 to 3 times farther than you can see ordinary, non-reflectorized objects. And this huge difference in visibility between reflectorized signs and most other objects may cause you to "over-drive" your headlights if you are not careful.

Of course lights on busy freeways and city streets increase your visibility. And you can use the lights of cars driving ahead of you to

Reflectorized Signs
The reflectorized signs are visible in your headlights from a greater distance than other objects. Notice that you can't see anything else around the farthest sign in the picture.

see the road far ahead. Nevertheless, over-driving is as dangerous as driving too fast around a curve or over a hill. By the time you see something blocking the road, it is already too late to avoid hitting it by braking. If you cannot stop within the distance you can see ahead, then you are in danger of colliding with anything in the road, such as pedestrians, barricades, and unlighted vehicles.

The best way to avoid the dangers of over-driving is to drive more slowly, especially on unlit highways and country roads. Driving more slowly will give you the extra space to see obstacles and to react.

Dealing with headlight glare

It can take several seconds for the eyes of a driver to recover from the glare of high beam lights. The length of this recovery period increases with a driver's age. During those few seconds a driver will be less able to see anything that might get in the path of his or her car.

For this reason, you should never look directly into the headlights of passing motor vehicles. This is not as easy as it sounds because your eyes tend to be drawn to bright lights. As you are driving along you need to resist this urge and look *up* and *ahead* beyond the lights of the oncoming car and slightly to the right. If the glare is especially bad as a driver passes by, slow down and direct your eyes to the pavement edge or road markings.

You can also help reduce headlight glare by keeping your windshield clean both inside and out. If someone smokes in a car, a greasy coating collects on the windows. And even if no one smokes in the car, there is bound to be some greasy build-up. The trouble is that no one ever thinks to clean a greasy windshield until they are driving at night and notice the glare. It is a good idea to clean the inside of your windows regularly.

Finally, you can protect your eyes from glare by keeping the lights *inside* your car down low. Dashboard lights should be kept very dim at night. And the dome light should never be on when you drive.

Using your headlights correctly

There are a number of legal requirements concerning the use of headlights. The first group of requirements establish *when* you must drive with your headlights on. They give set times (such as "one half-hour before sunset") and set distances for minimum visibility. Sometimes it can be hard to judge the proper distance or time when headlights must be turned on.

The safest practice is to drive with your lights on *all the time* and in some places this is required by law. Statistics show that drivers who drive at all times with their headlights on are much easier to see and are involved in fewer accidents. Even if it is not required by law, or you do not wish to keep your headlights on all the time, you should put on your headlights before dusk. This is a time of day when it is particularly hard to see and drivers' eyes have not adjusted to the poorer light. In addition you should always turn on your headlights when weather conditions are poor. For example, whenever you find yourself turning on your windshield wipers because of rain, it's a wise idea to turn on your headlights at the same time.

There are also requirements concerning the use of high beam headlights. Switch to low beam lights when:

— approaching another car from behind,

— approaching an oncoming car,

— driving on freeways or in towns and cities.

Specific requirements concerning the number of metres you must be distant from other vehicles to use your high beams are explained in the driver's handbook for your province.

Driving Manoeuvres

Nighttime driving is always more hazardous than daytime driving. This is in part because it is harder to see. In addition, people are usually more tired at night. Consequently they may be less aware of what's going on around them. This is especially true if they are driving past their normal bedtime. On any road, the combination of being less alert and being unable to see or be seen well can be deadly. The following tips are designed to help you manoeuvre your car at night more safely.

Turning

When you turn a corner or round a curve at night, your headlights will not be able to track the curve as well as your eyes can in daylight. To make up for this shorter sight distance, slow down more than you would during the day. A common driving error is to let your eyes follow the headlights. If you do this, you will not be able to spot obstacles in the path ahead because your headlights shine straight ahead, not around the curve. As you approach a curve, you

When rounding a curve at night, slow down and scan ahead and across the curve for obstacles outside of your headlight beams.

should always scan ahead and across the curve as far as you can see.

Meeting oncoming cars

A car's lights will often reveal its presence, even when a hill or curve blocks your view of the car itself. The lights will be visible reflecting off trees, poles, power lines, and water particles in the air. By detecting an oncoming car on the other side of a hill, you can change to low beams just before the other car appears over the hill. You may also be able to tell if the oncoming car is driving on the wrong side of the road. This will allow you to take evasive action in order to avoid a collision.

Unless the road is very smooth, you can get some impression of the speed of the oncoming car from the way the light beams move up and down on roadside objects. Lights moving up and down very rapidly may indicate either a bumpy section of road or a fast moving car. Also, lights get brighter as they get closer. You can get an impression of the oncoming car's speed by noting how fast the brightness increases. These crude speed-judging tricks might be good enough to tell you when another car is going too fast to make a curve. This would give you time to take evasive action or hang back from the curve until the other car passes through.

Passing

Be very careful when you pass other cars at night. If you have to pass and the way is clear, follow these steps:

1. Switch your headlights to low beam as you approach the car from behind.

2. To warn the driver ahead of your intention to pass, switch your high beams on and off quickly.

3. Signal, check your mirrors and blind spot, and pull out to pass. As you move alongside the car, switch on

111

your high beams. This will allow you to see more of the road up ahead.

4. When you can see the front of the car being passed in your rear view mirror, you are far enough ahead to pull back into the right lane.

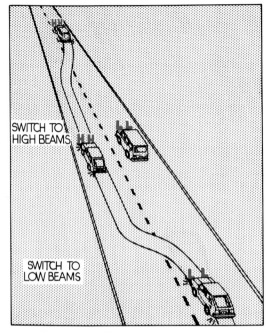

Headlight Usage When Passing

Driving in Rainy Weather

Rain is a contributing factor in car accidents. When rain first starts, oil and rubber dust on the road mix with rain water. This combination makes the road surface extra slick and slippery. In fact, a little bit of rain can be more dangerous than a heavy rain which washes the oil off the road after a while. Drivers think that because there are no heavy showers, they don't need to be as cautious as during a downpour. This is wrong, however, because the roads are slick when there is even just a bit of water on the surface.

Whether you're driving in just a light shower or in a heavy thunderstorm, all driving manoeuvres such as braking, accelerating, turning, changing lanes, and passing need to be done slowly and smoothly.

Hydroplaning

As the depth of water increases, tires have a more difficult job trying to cut through the water to maintain contact with the road. If there is too much water and the car is travelling too fast, hydroplaning can occur. In hydroplaning, the tires ride up on top of the water—just like a water ski. As a result, they lose traction. Control will be impossible.

The main factor which determines whether tires will hydroplane on a wet road is the speed of the car. The faster you are going, the more likely your tires will hydroplane. However, your tires *can* hydroplane at very low speeds. You can have partial hydroplaning at speeds as low as 50 km/h. There is no one speed at which tires will start to hydroplane. The only warning sign you may get is a change in the "feel" of the steering. If the tires are hydroplaning, your car will move in a straight line when you want to turn, and won't stop when you brake.

Three other factors which determine whether your car will hydroplane on a wet road are its weight, the condition of its tires, and the depth of the water. The lighter the vehicle, the more danger there is of hydroplaning. For this reason, heavier vehicles such as trucks and buses are not as likely to hydroplane. Also, if tires are underinflated or the treads are worn, they are more likely to hydroplane. Vehicles with extra large tires may be more likely to hydroplane. Driving into areas of deeper water on a wet road, such as puddles or standing water in worn areas of pavement, may initiate hydroplaning.

To prevent hydroplaning, remember the following:

1. Make sure your tires have ample tread depth and the right amount of air pressure in them.

2. Travel more slowly when the road is wet.

3. Be prepared for loss of steering control in wet weather—especially around corners and on curves. Brake before entering the curve.

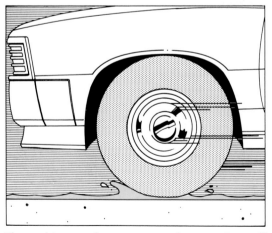

If you drive too fast on wet roads, your tires will hydroplane. Your vehicle's weight, tire condition, and the depth of the water on the road affect the speed at which hydroplaning starts.

Driving through Deep Water

If you can avoid driving through flooded areas, do so. Deep water can *stall the engine*, and *your brakes may not work very well when they are wet*. If you can't avoid the area, look at the cars ahead. Do they seem to be making it through without any problems? Check the depth of the water by looking at parked cars. Can you see their tires?

If you think it's safe, go through at a slow and steady pace. The water will tend to pile up in front of your tires. Go slowly enough that the water doesn't hinder the forward movement of your car. If an approaching car is going through the flooded area too, wait until the other driver is through before you go. The water will likely be deeper near the sides of the road, so straddle the middle. Watch as other cars go through to see which is the best route to take.

After you are out of the water, test your brakes to make sure they work. Try braking on a clear patch of road at a low speed. Did the car stop? If it didn't, your brakes probably got wet. Dry them by pressing gently on the brake pedal with your left foot while maintaining speed with your right foot.

Driving in Fog

At night or on damp days you may find yourself driving through fog. Fog is dangerous because it prevents you from seeing clearly and also from being seen. You may be able to see only a few metres in front of your car and may become quite disoriented as you drive. Use your low beam headlights to help guide the way, even if the fog is during the day. Do not use your high beams. The light from them will bounce off the fog and glare back into your eyes.

The most important principle for driving in fog is to go slowly and cautiously. Even if the fog seems light, you may come across thick patches. Never try to pass another car in fog. If conditions are very bad, pull over as far to the right as possible, park, and turn on your hazard warning signals.

While you wait for the fog to lift, if possible, stay in a place a safe distance from your own car well off the road. Another driver may unwisely be trying to travel and may accidentally crash into the rear of your vehicle. If it is not possible to get a safe distance away, stay inside your car and wait for the fog to lift.

Driving in High Winds

Rainstorms are often preceded or accompanied by high winds. Strong winds create driving problems for all kinds of vehicles. Drivers may have difficulty in steering, stopping, and manoeuvring. If you encounter strong winds, you should:

1. hold the steering wheel firmly,
2. slow down,
3. be prepared for any sudden changes in wind direction.

Even at low speeds, you may have to make large and frequent steering adjustments to stay on your path. Watch out for gusts near bridges, buildings, or steep hills. Any of these can cause sudden changes in wind direction and wind strength. These in turn can cause your vehicle to move from its path.

Of course strong winds aren't only associated with rain storms. They also make driving in winter snow storms even more difficult. Whatever the other weather conditions, strong winds can cause visibility problems such as blowing snow, sand, or loose dirt. If any of these are making it hard to see, slow down and turn on your low beam headlights. Strong winds can also spread snow, sand, or debris onto the road. This will reduce your car's traction. Look out for these dangerous patches on the road. Reduce speed and increase the space cushion around your car.

Driving in Winter Weather

Winter driving in Canada can be an unpleasant and sometimes dangerous experience. Drivers have to know how to cope with ice, snow, and freezing rain. All of these conditions lead to reduced traction and visibility—the two chief problems of winter weather driving.

Reduced Traction

How to get moving

To get your car moving from a parked position on a slippery or snowy surface, the main point to remember is to do it gently. First, make sure the front wheels are straight to minimize resistance. Put the car in drive or low gear. Push down gently on the accelerator until the car just starts to move. If you accelerate too quickly, the wheels will spin. If they do spin, ease off the accelerator. Try pressing again lightly. If the wheels of your car still spin after doing this several times, you can free the car by "rocking" it. To rock a car, you move the gears from forward to reverse and back again several times. Follow these steps:

1. First, put the car in reverse.
2. Drive backward slowly as far as the car will go. If you are stuck in snow, you will only be able to drive a few centimetres before the snow behind the rear tires stops the car. Hold the car there with the brake.
3. Next, shift to drive or low gear.
4. Move forward as far as possible. A build-up of snow will probably stop the front wheels from going any farther than a few centimetres. Hold the car with the brake.
5. Shift to reverse again and repeat the rocking, moving a little farther each time until your car is free.

If rocking the car does not work, you can try putting sand under the drive wheels to give your car better traction. And traction pads or even old pieces of rug kept in the trunk of your car are also useful in such an emergency. Whatever you do, however, do not spin your wheels. This will only dig them deeper into the ice or snow.

Driving along

Ice and snow are major hazards for the winter driver. During winter, the road will usually be grey-white. However, sometimes the road ahead may appear to be black asphalt. Be very careful. If the road is black it may be covered by a thin layer of ice called "black ice." And this black ice is extremely slippery to drive on.

There are a number of other ice and snow conditions that you will need to watch out for:

1. Ice and snow are more likely to be found in shaded areas. Snow is usually deeper in shaded areas.

2. Freezing rain will cover everything with a sheet of ice. Roads will be like skating rinks.

3. The closer ice is to the freezing point, the more slippery it will be. At temperatures near the freezing point, there will be a thin film of water lubricating the surface of the ice. Ice that is covered with a thin layer of water is very hazardous. You'll find this on sunny parts of a snow- covered or ice-covered road. As the temperature goes just above freezing, traction gets even worse.

4. Heavy traffic tends to polish ice and make it more slippery. This is true especially at intersections, traffic lights, and stop signs, where you need good traction the most.

5. Ice forms first on bridges and over-passes. Cold air gets underneath, causing the temperature of the road surface to drop faster than anywhere else.

To stop on an icy road, brake smoothly and well in advance. It helps if your car is equipped with snow tires or chains. Even so, you will notice how much greater the braking distance is for snow or ice-covered roads than on dry pavement.

115

One final tip: it's best to drive in the lane that has the least amount of snow, ice, or water. Try to follow the tracks of the car in front. This will give your tires more traction.

Reduced Visibility

Before setting out in the winter, you should make sure that your windshield, rear and side windows, rear-view mirrors, brake-lights and headlights are clean. In snow and freezing rain, use an ice scraper—perhaps with some ice-melting chemical—to clear all the windows. Clean off the hood and roof as well, so the snow can't fly up or slide down and block your view. Check to see that the windshield washer fluid bottle is full. If you plan to leave your car outside overnight and freezing rain is expected, cover your windshield with cardboard. This will save you a lot of work in the morning.

One typical problem in winter is foggy windows. When the air inside the car is considerably warmer than the air outside, moisture condenses on the windows. You can use the defrost feature on your car's heating and ventilation system to clear away the mist. Leaving one window open a crack will also help prevent the windshield from fogging up.

When conditions make your windows foggy, turn on your headlights. While this won't help you to see much better, it will make it easier for other drivers to see you. Other drivers may not be smart enough to keep their windows clear.

Seasonal and Emergency Equipment

Even a well-maintained car can break down under severe driving conditions. For this reason it is always advisable to be prepared. Some of the more common emergency equipment is pictured in the photograph below. How many of these items can you identify? Can you explain their use?

Useful equipment to carry at all times:
— flashlight or candle and matches
— basic tools such as screwdrivers and pliers
— flares or a red reflector
— first aid kit and blanket
— tire gauge
— car jack, tire wrench, and spare tire
— spare fuses (for electrical circuits) and lightbulbs (for directional signal lights)
— extra washer fluid
— spare accessory drive belt

Items important for winter driving:
— battery jumper cables
— shovel
— bag of sand or traction pads
— ice scraper and snow brush
— towing cable
— non-perishable food such as peanuts

Car breakdowns are never fun. However, if you are carrying the right equipment, you will be able to cope with them more efficiently and effectively.

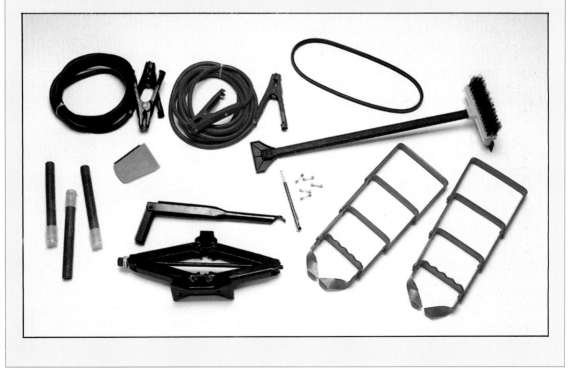

Winter's Coming—Snow What!—

Before you know it, it's here. Winter.

So it's time to think about "winterizing" your car.

First on your pre-winter agenda should be a tune-up. It will increase your fuel savings and ensure start-ups in cold weather. Also be sure to have these items checked:

Anti-freeze—If the concentration of anti-freeze is too weak, your coolant could freeze in sub-zero temperatures. Anti-freeze should also be changed every two years and your cooling system flushed.

Battery—Make sure your battery is completely tested and ready to go. If you think your battery might not make it through the winter, play it safe and get a new one.

Brakes—"Perfect" is not too high a goal for your brakes when you drive the winter way. Have them checked, cleaned and adjusted.

Tires—Your traction on winter roads will only be as good as your tire tread. Buy new tires if tread indicators are showing. Use your snow tires if you drive in snowbelt areas.

Windshield—Be sure wipers have adequate arm tension. Replace worn blades. Use an anti-freeze solvent in the washer system. Check that the defroster is working properly.

Muffler—Carbon-monoxide kills. A faulty exhaust system could mean disaster. Have the entire system checked for leaks.

If you're stranded in a snowstorm—It's best to know how to react in this type of emergency situation, because without this knowledge you could end up with frostbite or hypothermia.

The safest thing to do if stranded is to remain in your vehicle where you're protected from the elements, and stand the best chance of being spotted by passing vehicles or police. Use your motor and car heater sparingly to avoid carbon monoxide build-up or oxygen starvation which can occur in the closed confines of a motionless vehicle. Open a window a crack for ventilation.

By clapping your hands and moving your arms and legs vigorously, circulation will be stimulated and relieve muscles that are tense due to the cold.

Never allow all occupants of the car to fall asleep at the same time because you might not be able to waken someone from the frozen slumber.

Survival Kit—Always travel with a "survival kit". Make one up at home because good ones are difficult to buy. A small lightweight shovel could be just the thing to get you on your way when stuck in the snow. The smart traveller carries matches, and candles for warmth; a tin can or cup to melt snow for drinking water (avoid eating unmelted snow); a few chocolate bars or high energy food items; plastic garbage bags can be used to insulate against wind if you must get out of the car; and an extra blanket or sleeping bag might come in handy, too.

Smaller items could include an ice scraper, snow brush, flashlight, flares, tow chain, jumper cables, and a container of sand to provide traction to spinning wheels when stuck on ice.

Don't include alcohol in your survival kit. Alcohol causes dilation of blood vessels close to the skin, speeding up loss of body heat.

From the *Ontario Traffic Safety Bulletin*, M.T.C. Ont.

Extreme Cold

There are a number of practical tips for coping with conditions caused by the extreme cold in winter.

1. It is wise to use a block heater to warm up the engine before you start out.

2. Carry a small container of lock anti-freeze in your purse or winter coat pocket in case your door locks freeze.

3. Moisture can sometimes freeze in the fuel line. To help prevent this, use fuel-line antifreeze and keep your tank more than half full. The extra weight of a full fuel tank will also give you the benefit of better traction if you have a rear wheel drive vehicle. If you ever get stuck somewhere in a snowstorm, you will also be grateful for the extra fuel. It will allow you to keep your car running and warm until help arrives. However, under these circumstances do be sure to keep the car windows open slightly to prevent carbon monoxide poisoning. And do run your engine for only a few minutes every hour.

Slippery When Wet

Driving on Very Slippery Roads

Ice and snow, even in small amounts, always make control of a car more difficult and less predictable. Tires cannot grip the very slippery surface as well as an ordinary, dry road surface. On older road surfaces which have been used a lot, the pavement becomes shiny, smooth, and polished. When wet from rain, these pavement surfaces can be very slippery and slower speeds are needed.

The key to driving in such conditions is to drive smoothly. Bad weather calls for slower speeds, very smooth precise steering, gentle acceleration and extra care in braking. And, of course, increase your space cushion. It takes much longer to stop on a slippery road, and you may not spot a hazard as quickly when visibility is poor.

In most vehicles, shifting to neutral or de-clutching when braking on a slippery surface of ice or snow may give you better stopping control. This is especially true if the engine is cold and stuck in fast idle or you are travelling at a low speed.

Testing for Traction

Whenever you're suspicious of road conditions, you should test the road surface for traction. To test the surface, try the following:

1. Wait until you are in a safe area where there are no cars around.

2. Get your car moving very slowly, about 15 km/h, then de- clutch or shift to neutral and press down firmly on the brake pedal to "feel" for the traction available. If one or more wheels lock up, release the brakes and re-apply them more gently. If normal firm braking causes wheels to lock, then the surface is too slippery for good traction, and extra caution is needed for driving.

If, during these tests, your control of the car was less than perfect, you can safely assume driving on the roads will be no better. Remember, when driving on streets you also have other vehicles and pedestrians to contend with. So, if road conditions are really bad, leave the car at home and take public transportation.

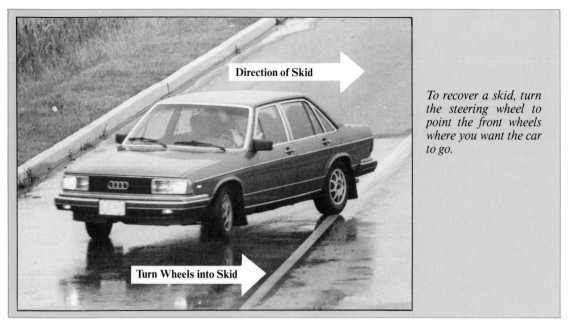

Direction of Skid

Turn Wheels into Skid

To recover a skid, turn the steering wheel to point the front wheels where you want the car to go.

Skidding

Skids generally happen because the driver fails to react soon enough to a need to turn or stop, and then makes a rough abrupt control movement. Skids can occur from improper braking, improper gas pedal pressure, or improper steering. The best solution to a skid is to avoid it in the first place.

A skid results from a loss of tire traction: the tires lose their grip and slide across the road surface. Skids can involve just the front, just the rear, or all four tires sliding.

All skids are caused by a "disturbing" force. Therefore the first thing you must do is to remove that "disturbance." This can be done by releasing the brake, getting your foot off the accelerator, and de-clutching or shifting to neutral *quickly*. If the car has started to rotate, corrective steering will also be necessary. Steer into the skid, that is, turn the steering wheel to point the front wheels where you want the car to go.

In many skids the car will start to rotate. In these skids if you haven't been able to recover steering control, the vehicle may

start to spin. In a spin, the only way you can have some control is to hit the brake pedal with all your strength. In this case, you want all four wheels on the vehicle locked. Once you achieve four-wheel lock, the vehicle will keep spinning, but it will travel in a straight line in the direction it was going, providing you keep maximum pressure on the brake pedal until the vehicle comes to a complete stop. (See chapter 8).

There are other cases where you would not want to stay off the brake. For example, sometimes when you are trying to stop on a slippery road, the car may skid in a straight line with the wheels locked. If it is alright to go straight where the car is headed until it stops, you might want to keep braking and let the car skid to a stop.

All in all, practice is the best way to learn how to handle skids: that is, practice under controlled conditions with a qualified instructor. Better yet, avoid skids altogether. Look up and ahead, read road conditions, give yourself enough time to react and make all your driving movements smoothly and gently.

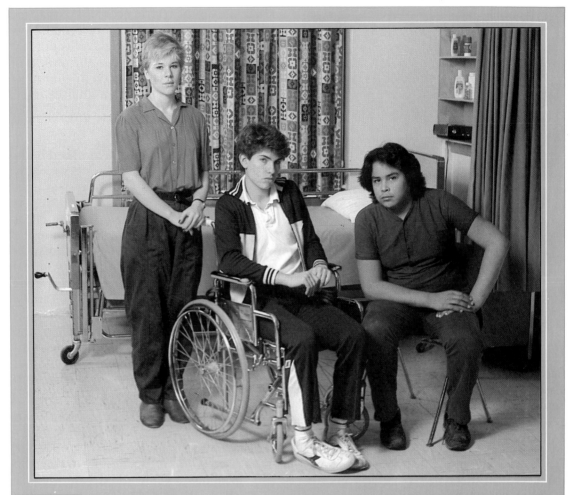

8

Reducing Accidents and Injuries

In this chapter you will learn:

- *about collision avoidance*
- *about the consequences of collisions*
- *about the importance of seat belts*
- *about the dangers of drinking and driving*
- *about other impairments which can affect driving*
- *about the consequences of traffic accidents*

Collision Avoidance

Good strategic drivers rarely get themselves into a situation that requires an evasive or collision avoidance manoeuvre. Why? Because they have been looking up and far ahead to avoid such situations. They've kept a space cushion around their vehicles, and they know how to read road conditions and adjust their speed accordingly.

However, even these good drivers may have to react to an emergency. What do you do if someone or something suddenly appears in front of you? This section describes some of the known techniques that can be used in an emergency situation. There are collision avoidance courses available where you can practice these techniques.

Making Quick Decisions

Collision avoidance requires the right split-second decision for the situation, and skilful control of the car. Do you have room to come to a controlled stop? Should you brake and then steer around? Or, is the only hope to stop as fast as possible? These are the decisions you have to make about what technique to use. But each situation is different. Do you have room to the sides or is there oncoming traffic near? Is the road icy or is the traction reasonably good? How dangerous is the potential collision: for example, is it a small child in the middle of the road; is it a truck stopped in your lane; or would it involve hitting a small animal?

To avoid a collision, you have three general choices of action:

1. **Threshold Braking** — Threshold braking should bring you to a reasonably quick controlled stop in your own lane, even in slippery conditions. Brake as hard as you can without locking up or skidding the wheels. Press down on the brake pedal, trying to get as much braking power as possible. Then, if you feel any of the wheels locking up, release the brake pressure slightly and re - apply. Don't pump the brakes. Continue braking this way until you've brought the vehicle to a complete stop. Some vehicles have anti-lock brake systems that give you a maximum threshold stop automatically.

2. **Steering Around** — Steering around an obstacle may be possible in some emergency situations. In this case, use the threshold braking technique to slow the vehicle down while you decide whether to steer left or right. Then release the brake and steer in the direction you've chosen. Try not to brake and steer at the same time. But remember, if you decide to move into another lane of traffic, make sure there isn't an oncoming vehicle, or one moving up beside you.

3. **Four-wheel lock** — You can use this technique when you have no other choice but to stop the vehicle in the shortest possible distance. Or, if you know you're going to hit an object no matter what, by using this technique you've done all you can to slow the vehicle down and therefore lessen the impact. To get all four wheels locked, you must hit the brake pedal with all your strength. And, it's important that

you keep maximum pressure on the brake pedal until the vehicle comes to a complete stop. If all four wheels are locked, the vehicle will slide in the approximate direction it was travelling when the brakes were applied. The car may rotate one way or the other, but its path will be a straight line if all four wheels are locked. During rotation, release of brakes could cause the vehicle to go in the direction the front wheels are pointing, such as into an opposing lane of traffic. For this reason, as well as to obtain as short as possible a braking distance, it is important that maximum pressure be kept on the brake pedal until the vehicle stops.

This technique gives you the shortest braking distance in most cases. Remember, when the wheels are locked you don't have steering control. You cannot, of course, use this technique if your car has an automatic anti-lock brake system.

Therefore, you usually have three choices in an emergency situation—threshold braking, steering around, and four-wheel lock. Shifting to neutral or de-clutching should help in all three collision avoidance techniques. If there is room, threshold braking should bring you to a controlled stop in your lane. If there are safe areas to the side, you may decide to steer around the emergency. If there's no other choice, the four-wheel lock can stop you in the shortest distance.

Collisions

If all drivers drove strategically and responded correctly to emergencies, there would be few collisions. However, as you learned earlier, there are hundreds of thousands of traffic accidents each year in Canada.

Force of Impact

Force of impact is the force of an object, such as a car, hitting another object, such as a telephone pole. In general, the greater the force of impact in an accident, the greater is the chance of injury or death. Three factors affect the force of impact of your car in a collision:

1. the speed you are going,
2. the weight of your car, and
3. the object you hit.

Speed

Force of impact increases as the square of speed. For example, imagine two cars, one travelling at 80 km/h and the other at 40 km/h. The car going 80 km/h will hit an object four times harder than one going 40 km/h.

Weight

The heavier something is, the harder it will hit another object. A truck weighing 20,000 kg will hit an object twenty times harder than a 1,000 kg car going at the same speed.

The object you hit

If your car hits a solid object like a large tree, the car will stop very suddenly and the force of impact will be great. On the other hand, if your car hits something soft like a chain link fence, the severity of impact is less because the car will take longer to stop as the fence bends.

Highway engineers now use several things to help reduce the force of impact in collisions. For example, smooth metal guide rails allow the car to bounce off rather than hit solidly. Wide roads, highway shoulders free of trees, and special impact cushions near bridges also reduce the force of impact. Sign and light poles are made to break off if hit.

The Human Collision

It has become clear that there are really two kinds of collisions within a single accident. The first is the car's collision in which the car hits something, buckles and bends, and then comes to a stop. The second and more important collision is the "human collision" which happens when a person hits some part of the car. It is the human collision that causes injury.

In a 50 km/h barrier crash, the front end of the car is crushed and comes to a stop about one-tenth of a second after hitting the barrier. Slow-motion film would show that the people keep moving inside the passenger compartment at 50 km/h. They continue moving inside the car during the one-tenth of a second that the car takes to stop. The people are still moving forward at their original speed when they slam into the steering wheel, windshield or some other part of the car. This is the human collision.

It is not easy to appreciate just how severe the human collision can be. To help understand what happens, imagine someone walking briskly head-first into a steel post. This would be about a 5 km/h human collision. The person would probably survive without serious injury. Then imagine him or her running full speed into the steel post. This would be about a 25 km/h collision. The injuries would be severe and the person might not survive. Now imagine the person's head striking the post at 50 km/h. The force would be four times greater than at 25 km/h and the person would not survive. In a 50 km/h barrier crash, an occupant strikes the interior of the car with such force it could result in serious injury or death.

Unbelted Occupant Dynamics

Car about to hit rigid barrier at 50 km/h with unbelted driver.

On impact, the car begins to crush and to slow down. The person inside the car who has nothing to slow him/her down continues to move forward inside the car at 50 km/h. Within $1/10$ of a second, the car has come to a complete stop. The person is still moving forward at 50 km/h.

One-fiftieth of a second after the car has stopped, the person slams into the dashboard and windshield. This is the human collision. It takes only $1/100$ of a second, so the impact is relatively more severe than the car's collision which takes $1/10$ of a second.

During a collision a person can strike the windshield, the windshield frame or a door post. All of these are hard and unyielding.

When a person hits something hard he or she must come to a stop over a very short distance, three to five centimetres. Because the hard surface will give way very little, the head and body must absorb most of the force of the impact.

When an occupant strikes a hard edge, a knob or a lever in the car, all of the force of the impact is concentrated on only a small part of the body's surface. For example, gearshift levers have been known to penetrate the skull and cause death. Severe injury from hard or sharp objects can result even in a relatively minor crash.

In a collision, passengers tend to move towards the point of impact, not away from it as might be expected. In a frontal collision, people in the front seat can receive serious neck and spinal injuries from being struck by rear-seat passengers. Vehicle occupants can bump heads with fatal force. In a side collision a person can crash into the passenger next to him or her and force the passenger out the window or door. During a collision people become high-speed projectiles, so it is not surprising that person-to-person contact is a common source of injury.

People often carry young children on their laps while riding in a car. This can lead to another form of human collision. Accident studies have shown that adults can crush their children against the dashboard during a crash. Even in a relatively minor accident or panic stop, a child can be pulled away with surprising force and hit the dashboard or floor.

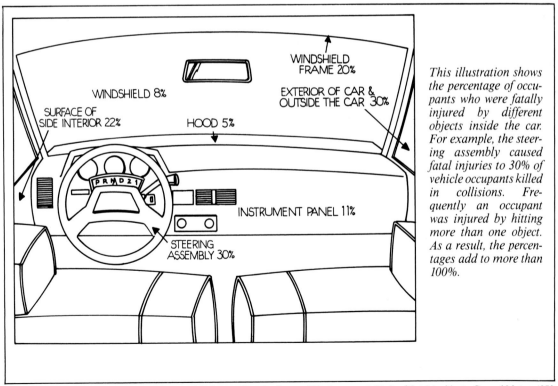

This illustration shows the percentage of occupants who were fatally injured by different objects inside the car. For example, the steering assembly caused fatal injuries to 30% of vehicle occupants killed in collisions. Frequently an occupant was injured by hitting more than one object. As a result, the percentages add to more than 100%.

Data from R. Wilson and C. Savage. Restaint System Effectiveness—A Study of Fatal Accidents. General Motors, 1973.

Seat Belts

Study after study has shown that the effects of the human collision can be reduced remarkably by seat belts. If you are wearing your seat belt, you become part of the car. This prevents the human collision in which you are thrown out of your seat by the force of impact. In fact, seat belts can reduce injury and death in collisions by about half. For this reason, in many Canadian provinces, the car driver and passengers are required by law to wear seat belts.

Myths and facts about seat belts

Even when the law requires them to buckle up, some people wear seat belts only on long trips or when weather conditions seem particularly dangerous. However, the statistics show that most accidents occur when the driver is only a short distance from home and when visibility is clear and the roads are dry.

Some people are reluctant to wear their seat belts because they believe myths they have heard. There are three common seat belt myths about which you should know the truth.

Myth 1

First, some people believe that seat belts will trap them inside their car if it catches fire or goes into water. In fact, this is very rare. True, a car might catch fire or sink in deep water. But your chances of staying conscious and being able to escape will be greater if you have your seat belt on. It only takes a second or two to unfasten a seat belt. You won't get out at all if you are seriously injured or unconscious.

Myth 2

Lots of people believe it would be better to be thrown clear of the car in a collision. However, the truth is that your chances of survival would not be very good at all. If going through the window didn't kill you, a hard landing may. And you always run the risk of being run over by either your own vehicle or someone else's. In fact, the safest

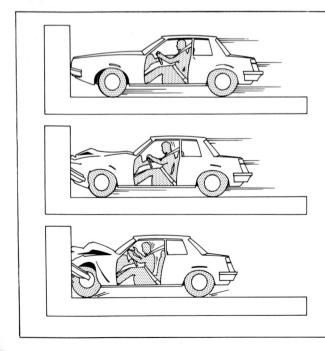

Belted Occupant Dynamics

Car about to hit rigid barrier at 50 km/h with driver wearing seatbelt.

On impact, the car begins to crush and to slow down. As the car slows down, the person moves forward until the seat belt restrains him/her. The seat belt keeps the person in his/her seat and keeps the head and chest from striking the car interior.

As part of the car, belted passengers are able to "ride down" the collision—to take advantage of the car's slower stop as it crushes and absorbs energy. For belted passengers, there is no human collision.

place to be in a crash is inside the car. If you really think it's better to be thrown out, ask yourself why motorcycle accidents so often result in severe injuries.

Myth 3

Some people believe that seat belts cause injuries. While it is true that belted occupants may occasionally receive injuries from the belts themselves, these injuries are usually minor. Bruises, slight rib fractures, and muscle strain and soreness are much more acceptable than the injuries which occur when vehicle occupants are not wearing seat belts. Any more serious injuries from wearing seat belts are usually a result of not wearing them correctly.

The proper way to wear seat belts

If your seat belt is not worn the proper way,

it won't protect you. A shoulder belt without a lap belt, or any belt worn too loosely, is of little safety value in a collision. The lap belt should be worn *low and snug* over the hips in order to prevent injury to the abdomen and pelvis. The shoulder belt should be *snug* across the chest in order to prevent chest and head injuries.

New cars have retractable seat belts that adjust automatically to your body. However, on some older cars, you will need to adjust the seat belts to fit each time you drive. This may be a minor nuisance if more than one person drives a particular car. But it is far better to take the time to adjust the seat belt than it is to risk severe injury in a collision. If a seat belt in your car is not working properly, don't drive until it has been fixed.

M.T.C. Ont.

Research studies of belted and unbelted occupant dynamics show that the belted occupant is better protected in a collision.

Child Restraints

In a car crash, children are more likely to be badly hurt than adults. Their bones are smaller and more fragile. For this reason, a child should never be carried in an adult's arms. A crash will tear the child away or cause the adult's body to crush the child. Protection for children is very important and is now required by law in many areas.

Babies under 9 kilograms should be placed in a safety seat that faces the rear of the car. Children between 9 and 18 kilograms should use a forward-facing safety seat. It belongs in the back seat of the car. Children between 18 and 23 kilograms can use regular lap belts. Children over 23 kilograms can use lap and shoulder belts.

A safety seat should be designed for the age and weight of the child and should fit your model of car. The safety seat should also have a label indicating that it meets federal government standards. In order for these seats to be effective, however, you must make sure they are properly installed in the car. Follow the manufacturer's directions carefully.

M.T.C. Ont.

M.T.C. Ont.

What Does It Take To Convince?

"Seat belts saved my life"

I'm convinced.

Although I didn't really need to be.

The ride I took recently in a seat belt "convincer" only confirmed for me what I already knew—that you're crazy to go anywhere in a car without your seat belt fastened around you.

The "convincer" looks like a giant cheese wedge on wheels, with a two-seat metal box attached to it in a rough approximation of the front seat of a car. The box slides on rails, pulled to the top by an electric motor-driven chain, falling back down with the force of gravity. It stops when it hits a steel post at the end of the track.

I limped towards the convincer, alternately clutching at my back, my chest, and looking for my appendix scar. But the officer in charge was not to be put off. He belted me in, the lap belt snug and low on the hips and shoulder belt loose enough to allow room for a fist, then flipped the release switch.

I'd like to be able to say, "and the car hurtled forward to what looked like my doom," but I can't. The ride down the slope was surprisingly gentle.

The stop at the end was surprisingly hard.

The convincer is designed to simulate an eight km/h or five mph crash, a very light impact in terms of what you'd face on a highway. But even at that speed, you're struck by the sensation of falling forward, of continuing to move after the seat has stopped, until the seat belt takes over and holds you back.

It's not a bad jolt at eight km/h, but it doesn't take much imagination to feel what it must be like at five, six, 10 times that speed, without that seat belt to prevent you from flying forward, to distribute the force of impact across your body.

The convincer is an excellent way of letting people experience, safely but dramatically, what happens in a car crash. So, I heartily recommend a ride in it to anyone who is still a sceptic about using a seat belt. I'm grateful I had the opportunity although, as I say, I was already a believer.

Why?

Because I remember a day in November eleven years ago when I was in a car accident. I was wearing my seat belt, and ended up with a cut lip, where I'd bitten down on it in the collision.

My mother, beside me, who didn't believe in seat belts, needed 116 stitches to close the gashes in her face and head after flying forward into the windshield.

It wasn't a very merry Christmas that year.

By John Russell, *Ontario Traffic Safety Bulletin,* M.T.C. Ont.

What To Do at the Scene of an Accident

As a driver, you have *legal* responsibilities if you are involved in an accident. You must stop and give all possible assistance. If you don't stop, you can be charged with failure to remain at the scene. You must also notify the police if the accident caused property damage over a certain amount or injury to a person. Check the driver's guide or handbook to find the reporting requirements for your province.

In addition, the law says you must give certain information to anyone involved in the accident who requests it. These people may include anybody who was injured, any witnesses, and, of course, the police. When they ask for it, you must give them the following information in writing:
- your name and address,
- the name and address of the registered owner of the vehicle,
- details of insurance including company, policy number, and expiry date,
- the licence plate number of the vehicle.

While these are the legal responsibilties, responsible drivers do more when they see or are involved in an accident. If you are in an accident yourself, or if you are the first to arrive at the scene of an accident, do the following.

Stop

Even if you are not personally involved in an accident, you are morally responsible for stopping if you see one happen, or if you pass the scene of an accident where help is needed. Park your car a safe distance from the crash. Be careful that your car does not block the path of approaching traffic or emergency vehicles.

However, it is dangerous to slow down or stop at the scene of an accident if police or other assistance has already arrived. Your curiosity could prevent the crash victims from being helped. Your curiosity might even cause another accident.

Protect the scene

Turn off the ignitions of the wrecked cars and put out all cigarettes in case there is spilled fuel which could cause fire.

The next thing to do is to make sure there isn't another accident. In their rush to help the injured, drivers often expose themselves and crash victims to danger from passing traffic. If oncoming drivers are not alerted, one accident can easily turn into a second one—or even a multiple crash. If you have warning flares or reflective warning triangles in your car, set them approximately 30 metres before and after the wrecked cars. If no flares or warning signs are available, at least one person should be positioned safely in each direction to warn approaching drivers. An accident scene is a dangerous place because of the risk of another accident. So be careful.

Make initial survey of damage

Now that there is no longer a danger of a second accident, you should survey the total damage—check the "human damage" first, then the "property damage." Look through the wreckage carefully to identify where all the crash victims are. Make sure you have not overlooked anyone. A victim could be trapped underneath a car or could have been thrown far away from the car.

Help anyone who is injured

Give emergency help to the injured in order of priority—that is, give help first to the person who seems to be hurt the most. Clear the person's airway to restore breathing. If necessary, give mouth-to-mouth resuscitation. Stop external bleeding by applying direct pressure to the wound with a clean cloth. Loosen the victim's clothing and cover him or her with a jacket.

However, *do not move* anyone who is hurt, except to save their life from fire, drowning, or electrocution. Moving a person with broken bones, internal bleeding, or spinal injuries can make the injuries worse, or cause death. Stay with the injured person(s) until help arrives.

Call for help

If help is needed, call for the police. They will arrange for an ambulance or tow truck if it is needed.

Exchange information

If you are in an accident, stay calm. You

It Doesn't Hurt To Help

In many situations we find ourselves relying upon our fellow citizens to help us in a medical emergency. Whether it is a doctor, firefighter, the police, an ambulance attendant or a passing stranger, it is reassuring to know that someone can and will extend a helping hand.

You probably have a natural desire to help someone in an emergency. But at times you may be afraid of what could happen to you if you stop to give help.

You don't need to worry.

The law is quite clear: Whether you have medical training or not, the courts expect you to do only what is reasonable, considering the situation and your skills.

What the law looks for is a common sense approach from anyone who stops to help another in an emergency.

At the scene of an accident:

- Identify yourself to the injured person. If you are a nurse, a doctor or a person trained in first aid, say so.
- If the person is conscious, ask the person if he or she wants help. A person has the right to refuse assistance and it is unlawful to act against the person's wishes.
- If a conscious adult or older child willingly accepts your help, you have sufficient authority under the circumstances to help.
- If a young child requires emergency medical care and a parent is not available to consent, you can provide emergency aid.

- If the person is unconscious, extend any urgent care necessary.

The law does expect you to be cautious when your actions could affect others. You do not want to cause more harm than good to the person you are trying to help. If the life of the victim is not in danger and you don't know what to do, stay with the victim, if possible, and send for help.

The law also requires that once you have accepted responsibility for giving emergency assistance to a victim of accident or illness, you must continue to give help until another person is able to take over—the desirable person being one with medical training, of course. The reason is that the person initially offering help may have discouraged any other potential helper.

There is no general legal duty to help someone in an emergency. However, in a few cases people do have a specific legal duty to provide assistance. One of the most important is the legal duty placed on any person *involved* in a motor vehicle accident. That person must stop and give all possible assistance to the persons involved.

GIVE THE HELP YOU WOULD HOPE TO RECEIVE IF YOU WERE IN SIMILAR CIRCUMSTANCES.

Excerpted from *"It Doesn't Hurt to Help"*, a pamphlet prepared by the Ministry of the Attorney General of Ontario.

will have to get information from the other people involved. You should get information concerning:

- the names, addresses, and telephone numbers of other drivers and witnesses,
- the name of the registered owner of the vehicle,
- the licence plate number(s) of the other car(s),
- the make, model, and year of the other car(s),
- the name of any other driver's insurance company.

To help you remember the facts of the accident, make notes. Draw a diagram showing the directions the cars were going and their position after the accident. Try to estimate what speeds both cars were going. Also note where the cars hit each other. Write down the date, the time, the location, the weather, and what the road conditions were like when the accident occurred. Note how much damage was done to each of the cars. Note the injuries, if any, of each person involved. When the police arrive, write down their names(s) and badge number(s).

You should not sign any papers. Make sure you do not sign any paper which gives a tow truck operator the right to make repairs to your car, or anyone else's. Be careful what you say. Most insurance companies advise you against admitting the accident was your fault.

If you hit a parked car, try to find the owner. If you cannot find the owner, contact the police right away.

Drinking and Driving

As many as half of all drivers killed in Canada were impaired from drinking alcohol. Impaired drivers cause many serious and crippling injuries as well. Therefore there are severe penalties for impaired driving.

What Alcohol Does to You

Alcohol is a powerful substance that alters the way you feel and react. It can have strong physical effects on your body.

1. **Kidneys**. Frequent urination becomes necessary.

2. **Liver**. Alcohol places strain on the liver and risks damaging it, if you are a heavy drinker.

3. **Stomach**. Inflammation or bleeding of the stomach lining may occur, as well as vomiting.

4. **Pulse rate and blood pressure**. Both increase with small amounts of alcohol but decrease as larger amounts are consumed.

5. **Skin**. Your skin feels warm although the body actually gets colder.

6. **Brain**. The normal functioning of most parts of the brain is interfered with. Communication between nerve cells is disrupted and small numbers of brain cells are killed. Concentration, memory, hearing, and sight are reduced. If you drink heavily, these faculties may be permanently damaged.

In addition, alcohol temporarily worsens your ability to think, see, and react effectively. Alcohol affects:

1. **Self-control**. Alcohol relaxes you. You may say or do things which you wouldn't if you were sober.

2. **Judgment**. Your ability to think clearly and make sound decisions is reduced even by small amounts of alcohol.

3. **Perception**. Your ability to see, hear, and feel things gets steadily worse as you drink. Even after one or two drinks, you may not be able to judge distances accurately and your vision may become blurred.

4. **Reactions**. Your reaction time gets longer and longer the more you drink.

5. **Co-ordination**. Alcohol affects your physical co-ordination. You won't be able to control your movements as well as when you are sober.

You can see from these physical and mental effects that a driver who has been drinking will not be able to drive as well as one who is sober. The sober driver possesses an ability called "attention-switching." This is the ability to scan the driving environment rapidly, interpret important information, and then make the right driving decisions. In many situations, the decision to brake, move quickly to another lane, or just maintain the same path of travel at the same speed, can mean the difference between living and dying.

Even after one or two drinks, a driver's attention-switching ability and alertness may deteriorate rapidly. Just a small amount of alcohol can make a driver "impaired" or less effective; concentration and co-ordination become worse, possible hazards go unnoticed, and the ability to make the right driving decisions and react accordingly is reduced. In other words, you need not be "drunk" to be an impaired driver.

The same amount of alcohol can affect two individuals differently. The outward effects of alcohol on a driver depend partly on personality and emotional state of mind at the time. An individual may appear calm and alert after as many as five or six drinks. Such a person may even appear to drive carefully. But appearances can be deceiving. That person's reaction time would be slowed down greatly, despite the fact that he or she looks calm, cool, and collected. It's just that some people mask the outward effects of alcohol better than others. A calm, quiet person can be just as impaired or drunk as a rude, loud-mouthed person. Don't let outward appearances—of yourself or a friend who wants to drive—fool either of you into believing that a few drinks won't affect your car-handling abilities.

Finally, it is important to realize that being emotionally upset or excited can magnify the already dangerous effects of alcohol. An angry person who has just had a couple of drinks is asking for trouble—or disaster—when he or she gets behind the wheel.

Blood Alcohol Concentration

Blood Alcohol Concentration (B.A.C.) indicates the percentage of alcohol in a person's blood. As you drink, alcohol enters your bloodstream. Your liver tries hard to remove the alcohol from your blood. Anytime you drink faster than your liver works, the extra alcohol stays in your blood and increases your B.A.C.

One thing that affects B.A.C. is how much you weigh. A smaller person can drink less than a heavy person to get the same B.A.C. If you eat before you drink or while you drink, this slows down the alcohol entering your bloodstream, so your B.A.C. will go up more slowly. However, *what you drink* does not affect your B.A.C. One drink containing 1 1/2 ounces of liquor, a beer, or glass of wine, will all have about the same effect. And combining alcohol with other drugs will further impair your ability to drive.

Drinking and Driving Calculator

Blood Alcohol Concentration

Refer to the Blood Alcohol Chart. Under the number of drinks and opposite your body weight, find the per cent of blood alcohol listed.

Body Weight	Number of Drinks								
	1	2	3	4	5	6	7	8	9
45 kg (100 lbs)	43	87	130	174	217	261	304	348	319
56 kg (125 lbs)	34	69	103	139	173	209	242	278	312
68 kg (150 lbs)	29	58	87	116	145	174	203	232	261
79 kg (175 lbs)	25	50	75	100	125	150	175	200	225
90 kg (200 lbs)	22	43	65	87	108	130	152	174	195
102 kg (225 lbs)	19	39	58	78	97	117	136	156	175
113 kg (250 lbs)	17	35	52	70	87	105	122	139	156

Subtract the per cent of alcohol burned up in your body during the time elapsed since your first drink, using the table below.

Your body "burns" approximately 28 mL (1 oz.) of alcohol an hour. To determine the effect of time on your blood alcohol level use these numbers:

Hours Since drinking started	1	2	3	4	5	6
% of alcohol burned	15 mg%	30 mg%	45 mg%	60 mg%	75 mg%	90 mg%

Example: Based on the chart, a 56 kg (125 lb) person who consumes 3 drinks in 1 hour has an approximate blood alcohol level of 103 mg%. After a two-hour time lapse his blood alcohol level is 73 mg% (103 − 30 = 73).

Driver impairment is reached before 80 mg% (commonly referred to as .08%).

Alcohol and the Law

It is a criminal offence in Canada to drive a motor vehicle while your ability to drive is impaired by alcohol or a drug or when your B.A.C. is over .08%. The legal penalties are substantial fines and up to six months in jail for the first offence. A second or subsequent offence will bring an automatic jail sentence and even stiffer fines. All such convictions carry automatic licence suspensions. It is also illegal to have the "care and control" of a motor vehicle when impaired. That can mean just sitting in the driver's seat, whether the car is moving or not.

It is also illegal to have opened alcohol available to yourself or any passenger. The police can stop you at any time and ask you to take a breath test if they have reason to suspect you've been drinking. Refusing to take the test is a criminal offence which will bring the same penalties as for impaired driving.

Even if your B.A.C. is below .08%, you can be charged with impaired driving if you are not controlling your car well. In some provinces, the law allows police to suspend your driver's licence for a short time, even if your B.A.C. is lower than .08%.

How to Avoid Becoming Impaired

The best way to make sure you won't be impaired when you drive is to avoid driving after drinking. Either don't drink if you plan to drive later, or don't drive if you have been drinking.

If you do drive after drinking, you are *always* going to be a worse driver than usual. Needless to say, you won't be as good at handling emergencies. For the average person, one or two drinks in an hour increases the chances of an accident; three or four drinks and the chances are doubled; five or six drinks in an hour and the chances are six times greater; and seven or eight drinks in an hour increases the chance of an accident 25 times.

Here are some good ways to prevent yourself from becoming impaired.

1. Drink slowly and space your drinks. Don't have more than one per hour.

2. Keep track of how much you drink. Measure the liquor input in mixed drinks. Mix your own drinks whenever possible.

3. Eat food before or while you drink. Food slows down the rate at which alcohol is absorbed into your blood stream.

4. Keep active. Don't just sit there and drink. When you are busy you won't drink as much. Dance, take a walk, or throw a ball around. When you start missing the ball, you will know it's time to ease up on the glass.

5. When you know you've had enough, stop drinking. Don't let anyone pressure you into drinking more and don't ridicule anyone else who decides to stop. Consume drinks with no liquor in them—no one will know the difference, or just put down your drink and walk away. There are always lots of unfinished drinks sitting around after a party.

6. Drink less if you're tired or have been sick recently.

Don't forget you are your own liquor control board. You have to know your own limit. If you realize you've had too much to drink, get someone sober to drive you home, take a bus or taxi, or wait until you sober up. The *only* way to sober up is to wait. It takes your body about an hour to work off each drink you've had. Nothing will speed this up. Fresh air, cold showers, exercise, or coffee may make you feel wider awake, but your reactions will still be those of a person who has been drinking.

Dealing with Impaired Drivers

Drivers impaired by alcohol may manage to keep their cars on the road and, if they are lucky, make it home. If they manage it a few times, they may think they can drive well when they've been drinking. Keeping a car pointed in the right direction isn't that hard. But doing the right thing to get out of an emergency situation requires quick reactions and co-ordination. Impaired drivers don't have these abilities.

Watching for drinking drivers

Whenever you drive, always watch for the other drivers who may be impaired. Some signs of an impaired driver are:

— weaving,

— driving too fast or too slow; driving fast and slow in spurts,

— overshooting or ignoring stop signs and red lights,

— passing wildly, coming too close to your car,

— stopping or starting jerkily,

— driving too close to the shoulder or straddling the centre line,

— driving at night with the headlights off,

— driving with windows open in cold weather,

— leaving directional signals blinking.

Preventing drinking drivers

As a host at a party, you have a responsibilty to prevent someone who is impaired from driving. You should be sure to mix weak drinks and have plenty of non-alcoholic beverages on hand. Don't force drinks on your guests. It may make you feel generous at the time. But how would you feel if one of your guests was killed in an accident because he or she had been drinking in your home?

As a friend, you should always watch out to see that the people you know don't mix drinking and driving. Don't urge your friends to have "one for the road." Don't press them to have a drink if they refuse or challenge them to a drinking contest. Instead, help them recognize that they've had enough to drink. If you are going to a party with a group of people, arrange for one to act as the official driver. This individual would agree not to drink any alcohol or take any drugs. Then he or she would drive the others home at the end of the evening. At the next party, a different member of the group could volunteer to be the official driver.

It is often difficult to prevent an impaired person from driving. Alcohol can make people stubborn and obnoxious and give them a false sense of confidence. If you know that someone who is impaired will try to drive away, hide their car keys, send them home in a taxi, or offer to drive them home yourself. It will be worth any abuse your friends might give you just to know they will not be hurt or hurt someone else in a car crash. If they are true friends, they will thank you in the morning.

Teens + Alcohol + Driving = Disaster!

Teenagers, like many adults, have many misconceptions about driving.

For example, although in general they believe they're pretty good, in reality it takes a long time to learn how to drive "well". So, it follows that they aren't experienced enough to drive and drink at the same time.

Alcohol affects drivers in many ways—some of which are not obvious. For instance, they may appear to have adapted fully to their higher levels of alcohol, but while behind the wheel, all their unimpaired physical skills and decision-making powers aren't available when needed instantly.

Fine motor controls and precision judgement are the key items affected by drinking. And the degrees to which they are affected is dependent upon a number of variables.

Being in poor physical condition, feeling fatigued or ill, can contribute to how well or poorly one drives. And poor driving conditions, decreased visibility, darkness and slippery roads heighten the chances of a critical error by impaired drivers.

Driver inexperience and the effect of mood-altering drugs in the blood, such as antihistamines (allergy medicines), sedatives (quieting drugs), hypnotics (sleeping pills) and tranquilizers, all work to further impair the already impaired.

The Traffic Injury Research Foundation of Canada has concluded that 16 to 17-year-olds are 32 times more likely to be involved in a fatal car crash if they are at or above a blood alcohol level of .095 percent than is the non-impaired.

An investigation by the British Medical Council showed that a driver's field of vision is reduced by 30 percent once the blood alcohol content (B.A.C.) reaches .055 percent. Potential hazards become difficult to detect because alcohol reduces straight-ahead visual acuity, distorts focus, reduces night vision, and alters one's ability to judge distances.

While impaired perception dangerously affects the ability to drive, it is made worse by the effect of alcohol on personality and judgement. For example: a higher accident-probability exists for impaired drivers who are normally cautious, because they begin to take risks.

There are four basic principles of good driving: smoothness, precision, concentration and discipline.

And if it's a difficult task to learn how to drive well when sober...and it is...then it's practically impossible when one is impaired.

From the *Ontario Traffic Safety Bulletin*, M.T.C. Ont.

Other Physical Impairments

While alcohol is certainly the most common cause of driver impairment leading to accidents, there are a number of other physical impairments which can lead to injury or death.

Other Drugs

Alcohol is the most commonly used non-medical drug and, overall, it causes the most harm to the most road users. However, drugs and medicines of many kinds can impair driving.

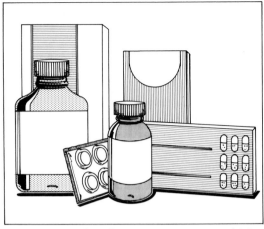

Many drugs and medicines can impair your driving. Even common medicines like antihistamines, antibiotics, and diet pills can result in fatigue and reduce your alertness.

Stimulants

Stimulants give the user a feeling of energy and alertness. The problem is they make a driver feel more alert than he or she really is. When the stimulant wears off (and it's hard to predict when it will), the user becomes very tired and may fall asleep. Stimulants include amphetamines ("speed," "uppers," "bennies"), pep pills, diet pills, and cocaine. Even coffee and tobacco are mild stimulants.

Depressants

Depressants "slow down" the nervous system. They ruin a driver's ability to think, see, and respond. Depressants include barbiturates (sleeping pills, "downers"), tranquilizers, antihistamines (allergy pills, nasal sprays), and narcotic pain-killers (such as heroin, methadone, and codeine), as well as alcohol. Many of these are found in small amounts in prescription drugs, cold remedies, and headache tablets.

Hallucinogens

Hallucinogenic drugs affect sight and judgment in different and unpredictable ways. The strong ones, like LSD, mescaline, and PCP can make the user completely unable to see the world accurately and are *extremely dangerous* when driving.

Cannabis products

Marijuana and hashish are cannabis products which distort judgments of time, distance, and speed. Like alcohol, these drugs can give the user a false sense of power and confidence. And, as with alcohol, you need not be "high" to lose your ability to drive effectively. A small amount is often enough to upset a person's ability to see, steer, brake, and make correct driving decisions.

Antibiotics

Antibiotics like penicillin and vaccines are drugs prescribed by doctors to fight infections and sickness. Antibiotics may produce undesired side-effects such as tiredness, headaches, nausea, dizziness, blurred vision, and itching. Don't drive if you get any of these reactions, or if you are taking a new antibiotic and don't know whether or not it will affect you. Always be alert for any side effects a medicine may be having on you. Ask the doctor or pharmacist who gives you any medicine what effects it can have on your driving ability. The same drug that saves your life in the hospital can kill you on the highway. If you have to take an antibiotic, you probably should not be driving in any case. The illness or infection you have will, in itself, make you a worse driver.

138

Taking several drugs at the same time (alcohol, street drugs, or medicines) multiplies the separate effects of each drug on your mind and body, and is *very dangerous*. The worst combinations are alcohol mixed with tranquilizers, barbiturates, marijuana, antihistamines, or pain-killers like codeine. The effects of any two drugs on your driving will be unpredictable. Some drugs in combination can even kill you. Remember also that overtiredness, anger, or excitement combined with alcohol or drugs will make you more vulnerable to accidents.

Fatigue

If you drive when you are tired, fatigue can creep up on you. There is no warning. Just a nod of the head and your attention goes off. Absolutely anything can happen when a driver falls asleep, and survival is just a matter of luck. A dozing driver risks not only his or her own life but also the lives of others on the road.

Falling asleep is not the only hazard of driving when tired, although it is certainly the worst one. Even if you don't fall asleep at the wheel, fatigue reduces your ability to drive effectively. You don't think quickly, you don't see things, and you don't react to them as quickly or accurately. In an emergency, you may make wrong decisions or be unable to make the right manoeuvres fast enough.

Highway Hypnosis

Driving for several hours on an expressway can be very boring. There will be few hills or curves. You'll be driving for a long distance at about the same speed. You may travel for some time behind the same car. All of these things add up to make you less alert, resulting in "highway hypnosis."

Highway hypnosis does one of two things. First, you become a "spectator" at the wheel of your car rather than the person who's doing the driving. You start to pay less attention to what's happening around you. Everything just seems to float by. Second, you may fall asleep at the wheel.

As soon as you start to feel sleepy, do something different. You can:
— open a window,
— talk to passengers or sing, or
— move your body a bit.

Stop at the first service centre or rest area and take a short walk or have a coffee or eat a light snack. If that doesn't make you feel any more awake, find a place to sleep for an hour or for the night.

You can help prevent highway hypnosis when you drive by following a few simple rules:

1. Don't eat a heavy meal before you drive.
2. Wear comfortable clothing.
3. Talk to your passengers, but not to the point of distraction.
4. Keep your eyes moving and check your rear-view mirrors often.
5. Take an interest in all road signs and traffic around you.
6. Take a coffee or walking break every hour.
7. Don't try to drive too far in one day.
8. Avoid driving during normal sleeping hours.
9. Keep the temperature in the car cool.

Health Conditions

In addition to fatigue, there are several other ways in which physical condition is important for driving. How well you see and hear, sickness, physical disabilities, and mental distraction can all affect your driving.

Vision

Your vision is obviously very important when you drive. To drive well, you must be able to see well at a distance, judge distances accurately, see to the sides, and see well at night. Most of the decisions you make when driving are based on what you see.

Many adults have not had their vision checked by an eye specialist since they were children. It is important to do so. The eyes change a lot during adolescence and vision problems can develop without your noticing them. About 20% of teenagers have some sort of eye problem. When was the last time you visited an eye doctor? If you need corrective lenses, you are required by law to wear them whenever you drive.

People who are colour blind cannot tell the difference between certain colours. Unfortunately, this means they will have difficulty in interpreting traffic signs and signals. For this reason they need to recognize the shapes of traffic signs and learn what the lights mean according to their position, rather than according to their colour.

Hearing

Hearing is important when driving. Besides being able to hear sirens of emergency vehicles, you have to hear trains and railway crossing bells, trucks, motorcycles, and other traffic noise. Such sound clues can be very important in warning you of an approaching hazard. For this reason, don't play the radio or stereo system too loudly when driving, especially if you have the windows closed. And don't wear headphones when driving. In some places it is illegal.

If you suffer from a temporary or permanent hearing loss, take steps to compensate. Leave car windows open a crack so traffic will be easier to hear. Leave the radio off. Leave the heater and air-conditioner fan off or on low speed. Make sure you stay alert, look carefully, and check your blind spots frequently.

Illness and disability

Any time you are not in perfect health, you are not in perfect condition for driving. Any illness or pain can reduce your driving ability. The medicine you take for sickness may have even worse effects. Whenever you are sick in any way, even with a simple cold or sprained ankle, you should seriously ask yourself whether your illness is likely to harm your driving ability. If it is, don't drive. It will be safer and more comfortable to wait until you are back to normal. Or get someone else to drive.

People with chronic illness (such as diabetes, epilepsy, heart disease) or those requiring continuous medication may suffer fatigue, spells, or convulsions. They should drive only if their doctor approves, and should avoid long trips and driving in bad weather. Some conditions may prohibit you from getting your licence.

Any time you are driving in less than perfect physical health, be extra cautious. Best of all, if you are not feeling well, treat yourself to a taxi or let someone else drive.

Distractions

There are several kinds of things inside the car which can distract a driver. Children, in particular, can be very distracting. If you are driving with children, keep them happy with toys so they won't bother you. Teach them that they must not bother you when you are driving. Keeping them in the proper safety restraints keeps children more orderly and makes them better passengers.

Pets in the car can also be distracting. It's best to have someone else ride with you to look after them. Most animals like lots of fresh air, so leave the car windows open. Don't feed animals too soon before taking them in the car. On long trips, stop regularly and take them out for short walks. The break will do you both good.

Emotional Impairment

Who would you rather take a ride with: (a) a driver who is angry and upset, yells at other drivers, accelerates violently as he or she swerves in and out of traffic, and is impatient to get home, (b) a driver who is in such a good mood that he or she hasn't a

care in the world, is laughing and talking excitedly to his or her passengers and not even worrying about the traffic, or (c) a driver who is talking quietly to his or her passengers but looking carefully around as he or she calmly deals with the traffic?

The Effect of Emotions on Driving Ability

What kind of mood you are in has a big effect on how well you drive. When driving you must concentrate on the road and traffic around you. Extreme emotions prevent you from doing this because extreme emotions reduce your ability to think and react quickly. Anger, frustration, depression, worry, excitement, even intense happiness, can all lower your ability to drive well. There are three important things that you should remember about emotions: they affect concentration and reaction time, they are contagious, and they are temporary.

Emotions can worsen a driver's *concentration* and *reaction time*. Any extreme feeling is likely to reduce your concentration on the driving task. It can impair your visual scanning and reduce your ability to watch out for potential hazards. Suppose another car moves out suddenly from a side street into your path. If you are worrying about that important exam tomorrow, you may not be alert to the approaching danger. Or you may not respond quickly enough to avoid a crash.

Every person is different in personality. Some individuals always keep their feelings under control. Other individuals become upset and excited very easily. If you are angry, you will be a worse driver; being calm makes you a better driver. Know what type of person you are and what state of mind you are in *before* you get behind the wheel to go somewhere. Make sure you are calm, fit, and alert whenever you drive.

Emotions are *contagious*. If another driver gets mad at you, leans on the horn and cuts you off the first chance he or she gets, you are likely to do the same to the next driver. But if other drivers are polite and friendly, chances are you will be a little friendlier to others too. Driving, particularly in heavy traffic, requires co-operation among drivers. If drivers are friendly and polite to each other, traffic will flow more smoothly than if drivers are angry and impatient. Don't be the one to start a chain reaction of anger.

Emotions are *temporary*. Any emotion, good or bad, will fade away. While you may be very happy, very miserable, or very angry for an hour or so, you won't stay bubbling, depressed, or in a blind rage for too long. Once the emotion has worn down a little, you will be in much better shape to control your car. If you do get worked up about something, wait a while before you drive. If you have just had a tough exam and are pretty mad about it, or if you have just seen a very funny movie and you are still laughing, don't be in a hurry to drive.

If you do drive when your feelings are running high, you may be impatient. You may drive aggressively instead of responsibly. You may take chances and make mistakes which you may regret later on. It is wise to do something else for a while until your emotional state evens out.

The Consequences of Traffic Accidents

A single traffic accident can change your life forever. And even if no one is harmed, there still will be legal, financial and social consequences to face.

Obviously, the most serious **medical** consequence of traffic accidents is death. But less serious accidents can also cause a lot of pain and suffering, some of it permanent. Some accident victims suffer brain damage, others are paralyzed for life, or lose limbs. Less serious but still painful are conditions like whiplash which may require long and costly hours of physiotherapy.

If an accident is your fault, you pay the *legal* consequences. If someone is killed or injured, you can be convicted of criminal negligence or dangerous driving. These are serious convictions, often leading to prison terms. Unlike ordinary traffic violations, these Criminal Code convictions remain with you as a criminal record.

The *financial* consequences of accidents are enormous. Medical expenses, legal costs, car repairs, and loss of work time cost Canadians billions of dollars a year. Even a relatively minor accident can cost thousands of dollars.

The *social* costs of accidents are impossible to measure in dollars. If a friend or family member of yours is ever killed or disabled in a car accident, the emotional pain can be enormous. If you are the driver responsible for someone's death, the guilt you will feel after the accident can last forever. Many people have their families broken up and their hopes and plans for the future destroyed because of car accidents. Don't be the one to do it to them, or to yourself.

142

9

Buying and Maintaining Your Car

In this chapter you will learn:

- *how to deal with a flat tire and a dead battery*
- *how to deal with mechanical emergencies on the road*
- *how to maintain your car properly*
- *how to save fuel*
- *about buying a car*

Maintaining Your Vehicle

There is nothing more annoying than getting a flat tire when you're driving in isolated areas at night. There's nothing more frustrating than finding your car's battery is dead just when you're in a hurry to get somewhere. Luckily, these two typical car problems are usually relatively minor and are easily repaired.

Far more serious are mechanical failures which cause loss of steering or brakes. Fortunately, most of these kinds of failures can be avoided before they happen. Regular service checks and periodic tune-ups by a reliable mechanic can help prevent these dangerous mechanical failures while you are on the road.

Some collisions are caused because of mechanical failure of one of the vehicles involved. Therefore there are regulations designed to keep unsafe cars off the road.

Two Common Sources of Trouble

Part of being a responsible driver is to know about the basic parts of your car and how they work. For example, you should understand something about what type of tires to use and how to maintain them. Every responsible driver should also know the safe procedures for dealing with common mechanical problems. Two problems that you are almost certain to encounter at some time in your driving career are a flat tire and a dead battery.

The Tires

Types of Tires

Tires have come a long way since the early days when they were made of wood or metal. Modern tires provide a smoother ride, are far less noisy, give much better

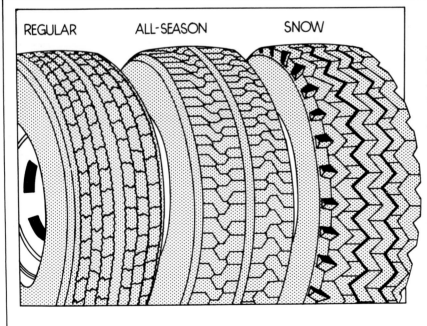

REGULAR   ALL-SEASON   SNOW

Regular tires are designed to resist wear on bare pavement. Snow tires have deeper treads designed to improve traction in snow conditions, but will wear more quickly if used on bare pavement. All-season tires combine features from regular and snow tires so that they can be used all year round.

traction, and reduce fuel consumption. Tires are classified into two main groups. The first has to do with their construction.

There are two basic types of tire construction: bias-ply tires and radial tires. Bias-ply is the older type of construction. In fact, most new cars now come equipped with radial tires. The main point to remember is that different types of tires should not be mixed.

Tires are also classified according to their use. And once again, there are two basic groups: regular tires and snow tires. The main difference between these types of tires is in their treads. Regular tires normally have five to seven ribs running smoothly around the tire. These give traction, but also resist wear on bare pavement. Snow tires have deeper grooves and the treads are broken up into smaller chunks or "lugs." These improve traction on snowy roads.

You should avoid using snow tires in summer. They will wear out faster than regular tires with a smoother tread. In order to avoid having to change the tires twice a year, manufacturers have developed all-season tires that you can use the year round.

Tire maintenance

For best fuel economy maintain the air pressure specified for your tires. Observe the vehicle manufacturer's recommendations regarding front/rear pressure differentials. Improper inflation can actually destroy tires. If a tire is badly under-inflated, it will become extremely hot. These high temperatures can weaken the tire and cause a blow-out. In the worst cases, the tire will come right off the rim of the wheel while your car is in motion. Similarly, over- inflation is also a problem. Too much air pressure can cause a bumpy ride. Your traction will also be reduced. And in extreme cases, over-inflation can also cause a blow-out.

If possible, check the air pressure when your tires are cold. If you must check your tires when they are hot, it is a good rule-of-thumb to add 4 psi (28 kPa) to the recommended cold tire pressure level. Check tire pressure once a week, or *at least* once a

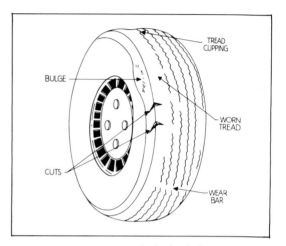

Examine your tires regularly for bulges, cuts, cuppings, wear bars, and worn treads which indicate that the tire needs to be replaced.

month. Include the spare tire in your check. Buy your own tire gauge in order to have a consistent measure. If you have the check done at a service station, ask whether the station air pump is accurate.

Worn tires can be just as hazardous as those that are incorrectly inflated. You must replace the tire when the tread in any spot wears down to 1.5 mm. There are wear bars moulded into the tires to indicate the minimum permissible tread depth. Some manufacturers suggest that you rotate your tires regularly. Check your owner's manual for details.

However, wear on the tire treads can give you valuable information. If you do spot uneven wear on the front tires, it means the front wheels need alignment or balancing. More wear on just one edge also means poor wheel alignment. If there is more wear on both edges of the tire, your tires have been underinflated for quite some time.

Changing a Flat Tire

Even if you've checked your tires regularly and replaced them before they're completely worn out, you may still get a flat tire. This could be caused by a puncture from a sharp object lying on the road.

Having a flat tire, no matter when, is a nuisance. It can also be quite unsafe to replace a flat tire if you're not sure what you are doing. But almost every driver experiences a flat at some time or other. So you should be prepared to cope with the problem. Therefore it is a wise idea to practise changing a tire when there is someone present who knows what to do.

Changing a tire involves the following steps:

1. Park your car on a level spot away from traffic. Turn off the engine. Put the transmission in *first* (if manual transmission) or *park* (if automatic). Set the parking brake.

2. If it's a front wheel that is flat, put a brick or rock *behind* the wheel diagonally opposite the flat. If it's a rear wheel, wedge the brick or

rock *in front of* the diagonally opposite wheel. This should help prevent the car from rolling as you work on replacing the tire.

3. Remove the spare tire and jack. They are usually stored in the trunk. Often the tire and jack are held in place by a butterfly nut that you will have to unscrew in order to remove them.

4. There are many different kinds of jacks. You will have to put several pieces together before you can jack up the car. There may be a diagram under the trunk lid or in your owner's manual that shows you how to put your own car jack together.

The diagram under the trunk lid or in the manual should also show you where to put the jack so it will lift the car safely. Put the jack into position. Insert the handle. Pump the jack up until it is firmly in place. But stop before it starts to lift the car. You will need the full weight of the car on the tire in order to complete step 5.

5. Loosen the wheel nuts slightly with the special tool supplied with the jack.

This may not be as easy as it sounds. The wheel nuts may have corroded slightly and be stuck firmly in place. If you have trouble loosening them, you may try giving the lug wrench a quick jolt with your foot, being careful not to damage the wheel nuts. Position the tool so that you can push down on it rather than pull up.

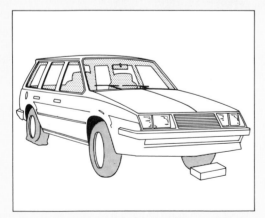

Correct placement of the block will prevent the car from rolling when jacked up to replace a flat tire.

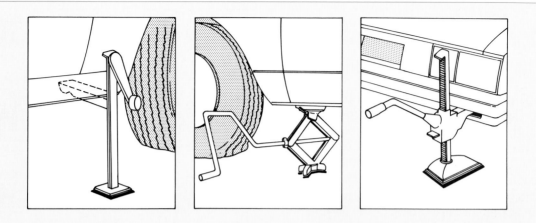

6. Once the nuts are loosened, you will need to jack up the car. Jack the car part way up so the flat tire is still touching the ground. Check again that the jack is securely positioned.

   Continue to jack the car until the flat tire clears the ground slightly. From this point on, you should be very careful not to get your body too near or under the car. It may roll off the jack, or the jack may collapse, pinning you under the car.

7. Finish removing the wheel nuts you loosened in step 5. As you unscrew them, be careful to place them where you will be sure to find them, such as in the wheel cover.

8. Pull off the flat tire. Replace it with the spare. In some cases this will be an emergency tire which can only be driven at low speeds. This kind of tire *must* be replaced as soon as possible.

9. Replace the wheel nuts with the tapered side pointing inwards and tighten them. Lower the car with the jack until the wheel just touches the ground. Then tighten the wheel nuts again. If the wheel nuts are loose, the tire could come spinning off as you are driving along.

10. Replace the wheel cover if any and put the flat tire and jack into your trunk. Remove the block from the other wheel. Then drive to the nearest service station to have the installation and air pressure checked. At the same time, leave your flat tire to be repaired or purchase a new one so you aren't without a spare.

As you can see, changing a flat tire can be a difficult procedure unless you have practised it first. What's more, it can also be dangerous to do. You may find yourself on a freeway which has only a narrow shoulder. In this case you should make sure all your passengers are safely away from the car. Light flares, if you have them, to warn approaching traffic.

Remember that the higher you jack up the car, the more unstable it will become. If the car is not on an even surface, or if it is on a soft surface, you will also have to exercise caution. If the car won't get high enough to clear the new tire and you're on an unpaved shoulder, you can dig into the dirt to free the tire. Otherwise, you will need to get professional help.

The Battery

How a battery works

The battery stores the electrical power which allows you to start the engine and operate the lights, gauges, and other devices on your car. It is made of metal plates sandwiched together in a rectangular box. Also inside this box is a fluid or "electrolyte" as it is called. For some batteries the car owner is responsible for maintaining the level of this fluid. This is done by removing the caps on top of the battery and adding distilled water as needed.

There will be two posts or terminals on the battery. One of these is positive and the other is negative. Cables connected to the terminals carry power to the various systems of the car. The posts and clamps on the cables connected to them can become badly corroded. This corrosion can spoil the electrical connection. Therefore, you need to clean these terminals with a wire brush every so often. Some people like to put petroleum jelly on the post and clamp assembly to help reduce corrosion.

When you drive your car, the battery is being charged as needed. This is done by the alternator which is driven by an accessory drive belt from the engine. You should check regularly to see that all accessory drive belts are not loose, frayed, or cracked. And if the alternator warning light on your instrument panel goes on, you should take your car to a mechanic immediately.

Signs of a weak battery

It's very rare that a battery "dies" without warning, unless you've left the lights on when your car was parked. You should suspect that the battery is weak if the engine turns over slowly when starting. Your headlights provide another clue. If they glow much more brightly when you "rev"

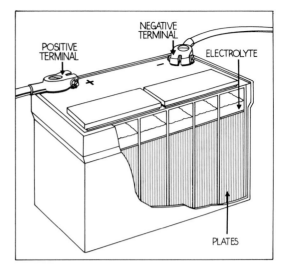

Cutaway Diagram of a Car Battery

the engine with the transmission in neutral, chances are the battery is weak.

You should also watch for signs of weakness if your battery is over two or three years old. While some car batteries have been known to last for nine or ten years, many only have a two or three year life span. In addition, watch for battery weakness in winter. Winter driving is extremely hard on batteries. First, it takes a lot more power to crank up a very cold engine. Second, there are often a lot more demands on the battery with headlights, heater, defroster, and radio working all at once. Third, even the newest and best battery won't work as well at lower temperatures.

If you suspect that your battery is weak, or if it is old, make sure you have it checked regularly. The mechanic at your service station can charge the battery for you and bring it up to full power capacity. You can also buy your own battery charger if you wish. This can be plugged into an ordinary electrical outlet overnight to provide power for your car's battery.

148

Jump-Starting a Car

If you turn on your ignition to the *start* position and you don't hear any sound or only a clicking sound, the battery is probably dead. You can start most cars with dead batteries by using jumper cables. However, if it is extremely cold, the fluid inside the battery may be frozen. This could cause it to explode when boosted. Therefore if your car's battery is the kind you can check yourself, unscrew the caps on top and check the liquid inside first before attempting to boost the car.

In boosting or "jump-starting" a car, you use two jumper cables to draw off power from a donor car's battery. Therefore if your battery is dead you will need to find a driver who is willing to help you.

Jump-starting a car can be a dangerous procedure. There is always the danger of an explosion. In order to lower the risk, you should follow these steps carefully:

1. Position the two cars so the battery cables can reach between them. However, make sure the cars are not touching. There is the danger of electrical current passing between them if they are.

2. Set the parking brakes. Turn off the ignitions of both cars.

3. Remove the caps from the dead battery if it has them. If possible, cover the top with a moist cloth. This will cut down on any explosive fumes or gases.

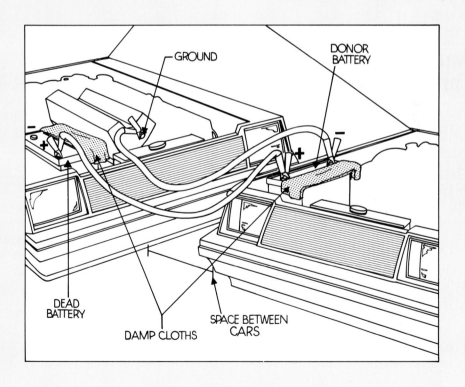

4. Find the positive terminals on both batteries. They will be coloured red, or have a "+", "p," or "pos" written right on them or beside them on the battery case.

5. Attach the end of one jumper cable to the positive terminal of the dead battery. Then attach the other end to the positive terminal of the donor battery.

6. Then attach one end of the second jumper cable to the negative terminal of the *donor* battery. Make sure at this point that the metal clamps on the two jumper cables do not touch.

7. Attach the other end of the second jumper cable to a clean, unpainted part of the *engine* in the car with the dead battery. Do not lean over the dead battery as you make this connection. Make sure the cable is at least 50 centimetres from the battery. *Never* attach the cable from one negative terminal to the other. This causes sparks which may ignite explosive gases around the battery.

8. Once the jumper cables are in place, start the donor car. Then start the car with the dead battery.

9. Once the car starts, take the cables off in the reverse order that you put them on. Let the engine run for a few minutes. This will allow the charge to build up again in the battery.

Remember that starting a car with jumper cables is not a permanent cure for a weak battery. If your battery is old or weak it will need to be replaced.

Mechanical Failures When the Car is Moving

If you keep your car in good shape and have it checked regularly, it is not likely to break down while you are driving. However, lots of things *can* go wrong, and you should know how to deal with *any* emergency. A loss of control, power, or vision while your car is moving can be very dangerous. It will require calm, quick, appropriate action.

In almost all cases of sudden mechanical failure, you will want to get the car over to the side of the road, out of the way of traffic. You need to do this as quickly as possible while at the same time avoiding a collision with other cars. Signal whether you will be moving either right or left to get to the side of the road.

Loss of Control

There are a number of possible mechanical failures which can cause you to lose control of your car. The most likely include steering failure, stuck accelerator, brake failure, and tire blow-out.

Steering failure

If the power assist in your steering fails, you can still steer even though the power assist is not working. It's just harder to steer. Grip the steering wheel firmly with both hands and exert more steering effort in order to get the car safely over to the side of the road.

It is also possible that the shaft and linkage joining the steering wheel to the front wheels will break down. This is very rare, but if it does happen you may lose your ability to steer altogether. If this occurs, all you can do is to hit the brakes as hard as you can to lock up all the wheels and slide to a full stop. In any case, if you sense a problem with the steering you should not continue driving the car.

Stuck accelerator

If the gas pedal sticks, you will not be able to control the speed of your car. First, slip your foot *under* the pedal and try to lift it. If this doesn't work, shift into neutral. Use your horn and hazard warning signals to warn other drivers you are in trouble. Brake to a full stop, and turn off the ignition.

Once you are safely stopped, you can try to release the accelerator. *Never* try unsticking the accelerator by reaching down with your hands while the car is moving. This action will make you lose total control of your car.

Brake failure

Poor car maintenance or replacement parts of bad quality are major causes of brake failure. Wet or overheated brakes may "fade" or stop working altogether. However, braking power will return to overheated brakes if you take your foot off the brake pedal for a few minutes. Don't "ride" the brakes down steep hills. This will overheat them. Use a lower gear instead.

If your car has power assist brakes, and the engine stops, *do not pump your brakes*. You should have power assist remaining for one, or possibly two, brake applications. If the power assist has failed, the brakes will still work but you'll have to push much harder.

It is also possible to have a part of the hydraulic brake system fail. If this happens, the brake warning indicator on the dashboard should light up. This type of brake failure results in a loss of brake fluid and the system will lose pressure. Most cars, however, have a dual hydraulic brake system so

you're not likely to lose both halves of the brake system at the same time. You will have some braking capability remaining and you should be able to stop the car, although it may take a longer distance.

If your car still doesn't stop, shift to a lower gear so the engine will help slow you down then gently apply the parking brake. As a last resort, rub the tires up against a curb, sideswipe a hedge, or even a guiderail. Hit something soft, like an embankment or snowbank, or head into an open field.

Tire blow-out

If a tire blows out while you are moving, let up on the accelerator. Don't bother putting on the brake. The flat tire will slow down your car anyway. Instead, you need to concentrate on your steering. There will be a strong pull to the side where the blowout occurred. You should be prepared to resist this pull to one side and try to steer the car in the direction you want it to go.

Loss of Power

Many things can cause your car's engine to stall or lose power. An empty fuel tank, a stuck choke, not enough oil in the crankcase, and not enough coolant in the cooling system are some possible causes of engine failure. Fortunately, most of these things can be prevented by regular car maintenance.

If your engine begins to fail or sputter, signal and steer off the road.

Shift to neutral and coast. This will keep the car moving long enough to get you out of traffic. Remember that the power-assist for steering won't work. You may have to turn the steering wheel hard. The main thing is to avoid stalling in the middle of the road. In this situation you would be a definite hazard to other drivers. Try to coast to a safe place on the side of the road.

A manual transmission car can sometimes be moved short distances even though the engine is not running. Shift to first gear or reverse. Then turn on the ignition switch as if you were starting the engine. In some cars the starter motor will crank the engine and the car will start to roll either forward or backward depending on the gear you have selected.

Wet engine

Driving through a deep puddle can splash water onto the engine. This may cause the engine to stall due to the electrical system shorting out. As soon as the engine begins to sputter, put on your signal. Steer safely off the road and turn off the ignition. Check for water around the coil, distributor, and spark plugs. Dry them with a cloth, but be careful—the engine will be hot. Try to start the car. If it won't start, you'll have to wait until the engine dries out.

Overheated engine

Slow traffic in hot weather, long steep hills, a loose or broken accessory drive belt, a broken water pump, a stuck or broken thermostat, a leaking hose, or a clogged or leaking radiator can cause overheating. Overheating can damage the engine. Usually the "hot" light or temperature gauge on the dashboard will warn you of overheating. Or steam may start coming out from under the hood. Do not drive farther. Signal, pull over to the side of the road, and stop in a safe place. Turn off the engine. Raise the hood to let the heat escape.

Wait for the engine to cool down. This may take an hour or so. While you're waiting, check the fan belt and look for loose or broken hoses. When the engine has cooled, carefully remove the reservoir and radiator caps. Wrap a cloth around each one first, and stand back. Steam or boiling water

may splash out. When it settles down, you can add more coolant to the reservoir and the radiator. You can add tap water, or even stream water if you strain it through a cloth first. Then put the caps back on tightly.

If the engine is hot, it must be running when you add the water, or the engine block may crack. A running engine helps distribute the coolant evenly throughout the engine.

Fire

Cars don't catch fire very often, but it's dangerous when they do. If you see fire or smell smoke, pull to the side of the road immediately. Turn off the engine and all electrical switches. Get all passengers safely away from the car. Try to put out the fire with a fire extinguisher, if you carry one, or by throwing dirt, snow, or a blanket over the fire. But don't spend much time doing this. If you can't put out the fire quickly, get at least 30 metres away from the car. The fuel tank could explode.

Loss of Visibility

Driving can be extremely dangerous if you suddenly can't see the road ahead. The cause may be headlight failure or hood fly-up. If any of these things happen to you while driving, pull over to the side of the road as carefully and as quickly as you can.

Headlight failure

If your headlights suddenly go out at night, slow down. Hit the dimmer switch and headlight switch to see if they go back on. If your headlights don't come back on, use the light from your turn signals, hazard warning signals, and parking lights to help guide you off the road. If there are no street lamps, you may have to rely on your memory of the road to decide on a safe place to pull over. If it's a clear night, the moonlight will help light the way. Pull off the road and stop. Do not drive any farther.

If your headlights start to dim, turn off any electrical equipment immediately such as the radio and heater fan in order to conserve whatever electricity is left in the battery. Drive straight to a service station if you know there's one close by. If there isn't a service station close by, pull over. Don't drive until the problem has been fixed.

Hood fly-up

If the hood of your car is not shut tightly, it may fly up while you are driving and block your view ahead. If the hood does fly up unexpectedly, don't panic.

1. Slow down quickly.
2. Bend down. Try to look through the crack between the hood and engine compartment. If you can't see through there, look out the left window.
3. Get off the road as quickly as you safely can.
4. Once you have stopped, shut the hood tightly. If the latch is broken, tie down the hood with a strong rope.

You can avoid a hood fly-up by doing two things. First, make sure that the hood is securely locked every time it's closed and that the safety catch is working. Second, check the hood while you drive. Do the edges of the hood seem to lie even with the body of the car? Does the hood vibrate? If the answer to the first question is no and to the second question, yes, stop the car and make sure the hood is closed properly.

M.T.C. Ont.

Preventive Maintenance

Regular checkups of a car are called "preventive maintenance." Preventive maintenance helps to protect the health of your car so it won't break down. This works in the same way that seeing a dentist twice a year and brushing your teeth every day can prevent them from decaying. Therefore you should follow the recommended maintenance schedule in your owner's manual.

If your car is not kept properly tuned and in good condition, it will use more fuel. Small problems, which *could* have been fixed easily in the beginning, will often become major problems costing a great deal of money to repair. Your car may even become unsafe to drive. On the other hand, a well-maintained car should go many kilometres without ever breaking down. A well-maintained car will make your driving safer. In an emergency, it may even help save your life!

Maintenance You Can Do Yourself

In the past, you could rely on service station attendants to do basic things like checking on your car's oil or the tire pressure. Today, with self-service stations, many car drivers have to make their own basic maintenance checks. There is nothing very difficult about making these checks.

The only problem is that some drivers neglect to do them. As a new driver it is important that you get in the habit right away of making regular maintenance checks of your car. The following checks should be done at least once every two or three weeks.

Checking the battery

If you own a maintenance-free battery you need only check the warning spot on the outside occasionally to see that the battery is functioning properly. However, if your battery has caps on top, you will need to remove them and check the fluid level inside. The fluid needs to be above the metal plates inside. Since the fluid level in most car batteries goes down over time, you should check it regularly.

If the battery needs water, add soft tap water or distilled water.

Checking the coolant

The coolant in your car's radiator helps keep the engine running at the correct temperature. Like the battery fluid, it, too, may go down over time.

It's a good idea to check the coolant *before* you drive your car. Check the coolant level in the reservoir according to the directions in your owner's manual.

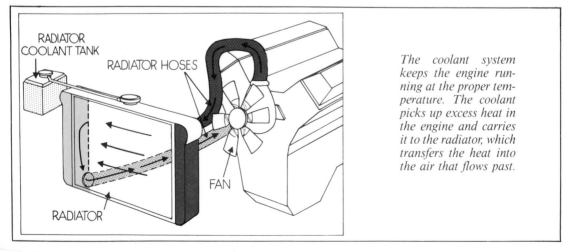

The coolant system keeps the engine running at the proper temperature. The coolant picks up excess heat in the engine and carries it to the radiator, which transfers the heat into the air that flows past.

Checking the lights

Any one of your lights could go out at any time. The trouble is, you may not know that you have a burned out light. Therefore, you should check your lights regularly.

It's easiest to do this with a friend who can stand outside the car as you test all the lights and tell you whether they are working. However, you *can* make these checks yourself. To do this, drive up close to a wall (such as in a garage) and turn on your lights. You should be able to tell from the reflection whether or not they are functioning. Do the same thing to check your tail lights, brake lights, back up lights, and directional signals. Back up close to a wall and check the reflections in your rear-view mirrors. You can also check your lights quickly by observing the car's reflection in a store window if you happen to be waiting in the parking lot.

It is not too difficult to replace burned-out bulbs in your directional signals or rear lights. And because they are so inexpensive, you would be wise to keep one or two replacement bulbs in the glove compartment. If you replace a bulb you thought was burned out and the light still won't go on, you could have a blown fuse. Look in the owner's manual to find out where the fuse box is in your car. Check to see that all the fuses are intact. They are just as easy and

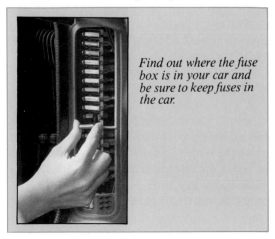

Find out where the fuse box is in your car and be sure to keep fuses in the car.

inexpensive to replace as the light bulbs. So, you should keep a few spare fuses in the glove compartment as well.

Replacing burned out headlights is a little more tricky. It is true you can purchase replacement headlights in stores and install them yourself. However, it is very important that headlights be adjusted properly. You can tell if your headlights are faulty or adjusted incorrectly if:

1. oncoming drivers flash their headlights at you while you are driving with your headlights on low beam,

2. drivers ahead adjust their rear-view mirror frequently as you approach,

3. your high beam headlights don't seem to light up the roadway far enough ahead,

4. your headlights light up the inside of the car ahead.

Any one of these signs means that your headlights need to be checked by an expert.

Checking the oil

Without oil, your car's engine would seize right up. Therefore, since oil can be burned up during regular operation of your car, you need to check the oil level frequently. Somewhere on your car's engine there is a metal rod called a dipstick. The dipstick is specially marked to let you know whether or not you need to add oil.

The oil can be most accurately checked when the engine is cold. To test the oil level, you should first turn off your car's engine. Then take the dipstick out and wipe it clean with a tissue or old rag. Reinsert the dipstick, pushing it as far as it can go. Pull it out carefully and look at the level of oil film on the stick. There will be two marks on the end of the stick. One indicates where the oil film should be if it is at capacity or full. The other marks where you need to add a litre of oil (or a quart in non-metric cars).

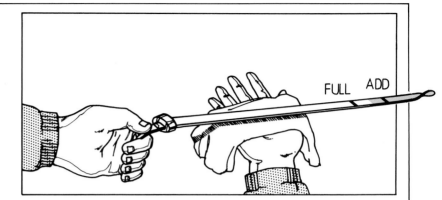

If the oil on the dip stick is down to or below the "add" mark, then you must add oil. If the oil is at the "add" mark, it will take about one litre to bring it up to the "full" mark. It is also important not to fill it above the "full" mark.

FULL   ADD

It is actually quite easy to add the oil yourself. And it can save you up to a third of the cost of having it done at a service station. Even supermarkets and department stores sell oil. You just have to make sure you purchase the correct type of oil for your car and for the season you are driving in. For this information, you should check your car owner's manual. Experts suggest you use a good quality oil and change it frequently in order to give your engine longer life.

You will need to find the oil fill cap located on the top of the engine. It is usually clearly marked. However, if you are even the slightest bit unsure about which is the oil cap, *don't add the oil*. Pouring oil into the wrong hole in your engine could have disastrous consequences. Check your owner's manual or have a service station attendant show you exactly where the oil fill cap is.

Checking the tires

As has been mentioned before, you need to check the pressure in your tires—including the spare—regularly. You also need to check for tread wear. You can do this by inserting a pencil or other thin object into the groove between two treads. If there is less than 1.5 mm of tread left, or the tread wear bars are showing, then you need to replace the tire.

Checking the washer fluid

Special fluid for windshield washers is sold in handy containers with handles and pouring spouts. It's a good idea to keep a container of this fluid in the trunk of your car. Then you can top up the washer fluid at the same time you make your other basic maintenance checks.

Maintenance Done by Your Mechanic

You should take your car to a professional mechanic for regular servicing and tune-ups. Besides these regular checkups, use your sight and hearing to watch for anything unusual about the running of your car. Does it make strange noises? Does it manoeuvre differently than usual? Are there drip stains under the car when it is parked overnight? These are early warning signs of trouble. You will need to have them cared for quickly.

When you do notice something wrong, don't just bring the car in and ask for a tune-up. The mechanic will have no other choice but to perform the tune-up, because he or she won't know what the real problem is. Your mechanic needs to know exactly what the symptoms of the problem are in order to correct the difficulty. Therefore, you should keep track of *when* the problem appears: when starting the car, after the car is warmed up, at highway speed, in a traffic jam, etc. Also, note what the problem *sounds* or *feels* like, and in what circumstances you notice it. Ask your mechanic to check those *specific* symptoms.

No matter how well you take care of your car, there are bound to be some mechanical breakdowns. However, your owner's manual, a sharp eye and ear, a bit of common sense - and of course, a good mechanic you can trust—will prevent many of your car care problems.

Fuel efficient driving depends on the car you drive, road and weather conditions, and the way you drive.

Fuel Efficient Driving

If you waste fuel, you are wasting money. In addition, wasting fuel causes unnecessary air pollution and damages the environment. Since the economy and the environment both affect the way you live, you should pay attention to how much fuel you use.

The Car You Drive

Some cars give better fuel economy than others. There is nothing you can do about this except choose the car you buy carefully.

In general, the lighter the car, the less fuel it uses. Before you buy a car, find out how much fuel it uses. Cars with manual transmissions generally use less fuel than automatics. It might be useful to talk to others who drive the same model you want to buy. You can also get information from consumers' groups and the federal and provincial governments.

Car options

Most cars have optional equipment. Options serve one of three purposes: they increase car "performance," they make the car more comfortable, or they make the car look better. However, most options also increase the amount of fuel your car uses. You have to decide what you want most. High performance engines, power equipment, roof racks, and air conditioning all lower fuel economy.

Mechanical condition

The mechanical condition of your car also affects its economy. Here is a list of maintenance precautions which will help save more fuel:

1. Keep the engine well tuned.
2. Keep the air filter clean.
3. Have the wheels aligned and balanced regularly.
4. Use a top grade motor oil and change it on a regular basis along with the oil filter as per the vehicle manufacturer's recommendation.
5. Keep tires inflated to the vehicle manufacturer's highest recommended level.

You can also save fuel by keeping your car as light as possible. Don't leave a lot of stuff in the trunk that doesn't really need to be there.

Road and Weather Conditions

Road and weather conditions will affect fuel economy. All cars use more fuel in cold weather, especially on short trips. Try to combine several short trips into one longer trip. Anything that reduces traction, such as snow, ice, or rain, will increase fuel consumption. You can't do much about this except avoid driving in bad weather. Regardless of the weather, you can save fuel by choosing your route carefully. Pick good roads where you can maintain a constant speed.

The Way You Drive

As a driver there are a number of things you can do to reduce fuel consumption, many of which are directly related to the principles of being a responsible driver and driving strategically.

Idling

If you are going to be stopped for more than ten seconds (for example, when waiting to pick up a passenger), turn off the engine. It will use less fuel to restart it than to idle it. There is no need to idle the engine for very long when you first start it, either. Once the engine sounds smooth, the car is ready to move.

In the winter, many drivers idle their cars for quite a while to "warm up." This is also a waste of fuel. True, the engine is more efficient if it is warm. However, in cold weather, it can take 30 kilometres of driving to fully warm up a cold engine. Those extra few minutes of idling won't make much difference. You might as well be moving while the engine is warming up. Half a minute of warm-up idling is enough. Your car will start more easily and run more smoothly if you use a block heater. Plug the heater into a timer which is set to switch on a couple of hours before you drive.

Climate control

The fewer power-drawing options you use

when driving, the more fuel you will save. Once the car is warmed up, leave the heater fan on low or turn it off. If the air conditioner is on, you will use 3 to 4% more fuel. The best thing to do is to run the air conditioner until it is cool inside, then turn off the air conditioner until you get hot again. Using upper vents instead of opening windows or using the air conditioner can save 2% on fuel.

Driving strategically

Driving strategically involves, among other things, anticipating changes that are about to occur in the driving situation and being ready to respond to them well in advance. This leads to smooth and precise control of the car. And this, in turn, leads to fuel-efficient driving.

For example, strategic driving involves gentle acceleration with constant pressure on the gas pedal. Jack-rabbit starts or stomping on the accelerator will only use extra fuel. Strategic driving also involves maintaining the common speed and noticing well in advance when your speed will need to change. Changing speed almost always uses extra fuel or wastes it. By anticipating the need to change speed, the driver can do so gently and therefore save fuel. As an example, removing your foot from the gas pedal and coasting to a gentle stop is far more fuel-efficient than slamming on the brakes.

Being a responsible driver

Being a responsible driver involves, in part, obeying the rules of the road. This can have a significant effect on fuel efficiency when it comes to speed limits. At highway speeds, in particular, the faster you drive, the more fuel it takes to travel the same distance. For example, it takes approximately 20% more fuel if you travel at 110 km/h instead of at 90 km/h. This fact is just one more good reason why you should always obey speed limits.

Buying a Car

What are the costs of owning a car?

Cars are expensive, even used cars. For a car to be worth owning and operating, it has to be in good condition, and that means it's going to be costly. But the cost of a car doesn't stop with what's written on the windshield price tag. After you've paid the tax, dealer service charges, and licensing fees, you still have to pay for insurance before you can drive it. Then you have to pay for the maintenance (oil, lubrication, filters, wheel alignment, tuneups), repairs (no car is perfect), and any special features you can't live without (like sound systems).

Unless you have enough money to pay cash for your car, you're going to have to finance it. That means monthly payments, and paying a lot of money in loan interest. Make sure you can afford the payments before you buy. So look at the *total* cost. Of course, you also have to pay for fuel and parking. Remember, when you buy a car, you commit yourself to a lot of future expenses. What else could you buy with that money? If you decide to buy a car, buy wisely!

What kind of car should you buy?

Which car to buy is a big decision. Remember that a car is an investment. You want it to still be worth something when you sell it or trade it in. Some cars have a much higher resale value than others. These days, the amount of fuel a car uses is a big factor in its resale value. Check the *Transport Canada Fuel Consumption Guide*, available from the federal Department of Transport. It will tell you how fuel-efficient various makes and models of cars are. If you choose an imported car or a used model that is no longer made, make sure you can get parts and servicing wherever you are likely to drive. Various consumer associations keep records of repairs each car needs. In general, read as many government pamphlets and consumer publications as you can before deciding on what kind of car you want to buy.

Buying a new car

Fuel economy, safety features, reputation of the manufacturer, and cost are things to consider when buying a new car. You pay a lot of money for a new car, and it's worth less as soon as you drive it off the lot. However the advantage of buying a new car is that it comes with a warranty or guarantee. If anything goes wrong over the first several thousand kilometres, you are protected from paying for costly repairs. New cars are also less likely to break down and you should have little or no trouble getting parts for them.

Buying a used car

Buying a used car is tricky. First, you should check price trends in the newspaper to find out approximately what used cars cost. Make sure that the car you get is just "used," not "used-up."

Don't believe everything you are told about a used car until you check it out for yourself. If buying privately, size up the seller as well as the car. How well do you think the car has been driven and maintained? Don't be afraid to ask questions and check the car over thoroughly. Try to get an idea of the condition of the engine, body, transmission, exhaust, suspension, cooling and electrical systems, brakes, and fuel economy. Check for leaks under the car and for uneven tire wear. Remember that the odometer on a car is not foolproof - it may have been set back to make you think the car has fewer kilometres on it than it really does (although this is against the law). Take the car for a test drive to see how well it handles.

Once you have decided on the used car you want to buy, the safest thing is to hire a mechanic to look over the car. It will cost you a few dollars, but could save you from buying a "lemon." Also, you should check for liens against the car with your provincial government agency.

There are several books available on buying used cars. Read up and know what you're doing.

Motor Vehicle Registration and Inspection

A car, like all other motor vehicles, must be registered by the owner with the provincial transportation authorities before it can be driven. The vehicle permit must be carried in the car.

It is against the law to drive a car that is in a mechanically unsafe condition. If a car is suspected to be mechanically unsafe by police, the car may have to be submitted for an inspection. The car may be removed from the road until the defect is fixed.

When a used car changes owners, many provinces require that it receive a checkup or inspection. In some provinces police do spotchecks on cars that don't seem to be working properly. These checks and inspections help prevent serious accidents by helping to ensure that all cars on the road are in safe mechanical condition.

Conclusion

This book has tried to teach you the principles of being a responsible driver and of driving strategically. If you have learned these lessons well and practise them consistently whenever you are on the road, you should have a long, safe, and pleasurable driving career. One final comment. As a new driver, you're still probably feeling quite nervous at the wheel. However, no matter how experienced a driver you become, you should always remain alert to danger. Over-confidence is perhaps the worst enemy of all.

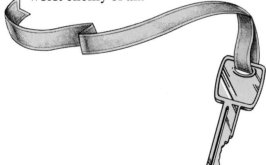

Index

Note: *Illustrations are indicated by page numbers in* **boldface.**